W9-DET-961

Happy Starts at Home

Getting the Life You Want by Changing the Space You've Got

Rebecca West

Booktrope Editions

Seattle WA 2016

Cover Design by Michelle Fairbanks/Fresh Design

Names and identifying details of some of the people portrayed in this book have been changed.

Print ISBN 978-1-5137-0667-2

EPUB ISBN 978-1-5137-0768-6

Library of Congress Control Number: 2016900836

Acknowledgments

To Terry and Jack, and to Tom and Linda. To Kelly, Carolyn, Emily, and most especially Damian. For showing me how to make a house a home, for teaching me to think positively, for helping me listen to my intuition, and for encouraging me to let the sparkle show. Thank you.

Contents

Introduction

"When you get your house in order, other
parts of your life just start to follow."
—Maxwell Gillingham-Ryan

THIS BOOK IS ABOUT USING your home as a tool to *make change happen in your life.*

Your home can be the key to better health, better sleep, better relationships, and an all-around better life. Your home can also lock you into a damaging relationship, drain your energy, and devour your money. Every choice you make about your home influences your life. With every dollar you spend on your home, you cast a vote for the kind of life you wish to live: what you value, how you will be treated, and whom you will let in. It's *that* powerful!

If you're like me, you are highly affected by your environment. In a messy room we feel frustrated, stressed, even out of control. We crave the beauty and calm depicted in glossy home decorating magazines—not just because the pictures are pretty, but because we imagine that if we could just get our homes close to that ideal, we'd enjoy less stressful, more contented lives.

The truth is your home *can* directly improve your well-being and contentment. It *can* help decrease your stress level and increase your happiness. But not necessarily by looking like the cover of *Architectural Digest*.

HAPPY STARTS AT HOME™

I became a designer by chance, not by, well, design. Nearly a decade ago I found myself divorced and living in a house that constantly reminded me of my failed marriage. Later I'll share more of my story, but for now let me summarize it this way: I got tired of living in a house that reverberated with sadness, loss, and defeat.

After about six months of feeling stuck, I repainted the walls and completely refurnished the house. (No, it didn't take buckets of money. More on that in the chapters to follow.) Here's what I discovered: changing what I saw around me transformed how I saw my future. And that change thrilled me. While I hadn't physically moved, I had psychologically moved on.

I started my design company because I am passionate about helping other people experience the transformative power of the home. I feel a special connection to folks who are in life transition (like divorce or empty-nesting) or who may feel blocked, frustrated, or trapped, like I once did. So, while I did go back to school to earn a degree in interior design, I didn't start my company out of a love for design per se. I started it to help people use their home as a tool for change. To this day I don't really care if you buy a new sofa. I do care that your home is working for you.

It's not about buying or not buying a new sofa. It's about whether your home is working for you.

I want to share with you the tools you need to create your own happy home. It's not a matter of copying design trends. It's a matter of figuring out what you need from your home, and then identifying how to make it work for you.

FIRST, LET'S ASK *WHY*.

A lot of books out there tell you *how* to declutter, decorate, and design your home, but many skip the most important question—*why*? **Why have you decided to change something about your home? Why spend your time, money, and energy decorating or remodeling? What outcome do you seek?**

Maybe the answers seem obvious to you, but let me probe a little more deeply: **Who are you making changes for? What do you hope will happen by making these changes and spending this money? What outcome must be realized for all of the expense, stress, and time to have been worth it? How will you know you've succeeded?**

If you haven't really examined—and answered—the important questions before diving into a home remodel or decorating project, you may:

- End up with a beautifully remodeled kitchen that fails to function for your family.
- Start out strong but eventually lose motivation and remain stuck in a cluttered, shabby, dysfunctional home.
- Create a picture-perfect home but realize that nothing has really changed in your life.

When you make changes without focus and intention, you *might* hit a bull's-eye, but it'll just be luck. When you don't know what you are aiming at, you have a slim chance of hitting the target: you are much more likely to miss. You'll have spent a lot of money and endured a lot of stress but, in the end, failed to succeed.

When we aren't driven by a clear and *internal* motivating factor to implement change, the change (if we achieve it at all) rarely lasts. Like a person who loses weight to please someone else or who loses it too quickly and gains it all right back, your house ends up (or stays) out of shape. The answer to "Why should you invest in your home?" is this: You shouldn't! Not unless that investment results in a home in which you feel more carefree, confident, and cared for, and not unless you know why *you* (not your mom or your sister or your friend) will be happier as a result. If the stress of a home remodel doesn't produce a positive life outcome, you'd be better off spending your money on a trip to Italy or your time playing with your dog.

I know that's a lot of high-minded "self-helpy" talk, so let's get practical for a moment. In fact, here's a personal example of a positive life outcome. When I married for the second time, my fiancé and I decided that if we were going to spend thousands on a wedding, we might as well get something long lasting from it (I mean, besides a marriage, of course!). We enjoy hosting parties and barbecues, and we also have a passion for ballroom dance and dreamed of hosting dancing parties and lessons at our home. Inside, our modest house could accommodate, at most, about a dozen people, but outside, our giant weedy-sloped backyard was ripe with potential. We decided to host the wedding at our home and invest in revamping the backyard into a terraced entertaining space.

Be warned, this kind of undertaking is not for the faint of heart. Think long and hard before you plan a wedding and remodel your home at the same time. But for us, it was the right choice. Was it stressful? You bet! Was it exhausting? Yep! Was it expensive? Oh yeah. Was it worth it? Absolutely!

By focusing on an end goal we are able to create spaces that enrich our lives.

In the year after our wedding, we hosted another half-dozen outdoor soirées, including a zombie-apocalypse emergency planning party and an auction for my local Toastmasters club. That was the prize on which we'd kept our eye the whole time we were neck deep in wedding and remodeling chaos. We stuck with it because we knew we'd end up with an outdoor space that suited our lives. Visualizing our goal helped us keep perspective and make good long-term decisions. And because we understood our end goal, our *why*, we ended up with a space that really did enrich our lives. (Throwing a half-dozen outdoor parties in rainy Seattle is really saying something!)

Here's the thing: you shouldn't spend money to remodel or redecorate unless you understand the meaning and intention behind it. That would be like packing for a vacation without knowing your destination. You'd either pack too much or too little, and either way likely not have what you need when you got there. This book can help you clarify what you need from your home and identify how it can better support your life, dreams, and goals. I want you to be able to remodel or redecorate with clear intent, avoid wasting your money, and have confidence that the outcome will have been worth the effort.

So how about you? How can you set an intentional goal for your space and project? How can you make decisions for your remodel and have confidence that you are making the right calls? How can you use your home to achieve more joy, calm, love, and success in your life? How can you get—and stay—happier at home?

WELL, WHAT IS IT YOU *REALLY* WANT?

It's a matter of figuring out what you *really* want. Not a "new kitchen" but "more healthy home-cooked meals to help my diabetic partner live longer." Not a "prettier living room" but a "space where I can spend more time with my friends and family." If you can identify your desires at a core-values level, then you can assess what you need to change to achieve those goals, and then collect the right "tools" to make those goals a reality.

Yes, the spaces matter, because *they are the tools*. A functional kitchen makes it possible to cook healthy meals at home. A comfortable living room makes it possible to hang out in the space with friends. It's just like setting a goal to run a marathon. To run 26.2 miles you have to wear comfortable, well-fitting shoes. It would be silly to think you could succeed if you hit the road wearing shoes that didn't fit, right? The same thinking applies to your home. If you want to run the marathon of life to the best of your ability but you spend your days in a home or work environment that is the wrong fit, how can you expect to perform at your peak? For a marathon, you wouldn't go out and just buy a random pair of pretty shoes. First, you'd set a goal to run a marathon, and *then* you'd buy the *right* shoes for the job. So before you start to redecorate or remodel, you must connect with your core values, see your surroundings with new eyes, and understand how your home supports (or sabotages) the things, people, and activities you most value. Only when you understand the profound impact that your home has in giving you (or keeping you from) the life you crave can you identify how you *want* to live, come up with a concrete *why* to guide your successful project, and create a plan to get to your new life.

It is essential that we know our "why" before we make changes to our homes. When we are not deeply connected to a defined intention, we tend to go through the motions, avoid the hard decisions, and miss key changes that would have made a huge impact. To make matters worse, without that clear and achievable target, we don't have any way of knowing when we are *done*. *Following the latest trend just isn't enough.* With any home project we have to connect to an intention, a purpose, that will serve our life.

101 USES FOR WALLPAPER? NO!

This book isn't an interior design how-to guide. This book is about aligning your heart, your home, and your health. It's about getting a geographical cure (putting yourself in a new environment) without actually relocating.

It is about creating a home that will nurture and support the life you deserve to live. If you plan to redecorate, this book will help you identify and buy what you need to feel your best in your space. If you are about to remodel, the activities in this book will better equip you to communicate your needs to an architect, a designer, or a contractor, and will help ensure that you end up with the home, and life, of your dreams. This is important because I want you to have the home of *your* dreams, not the home of your designer's dreams.

You should have the home of *your* dreams, not your designer's dreams.

PERFECT ISN'T ENOUGH. IT'S NOT EVEN NECESSARY.

We're lucky to have access to many beautiful things for our homes. Throughout history only the rich and famous had stylish and luxurious homes, but now the modern American family can choose from a rainbow of paint colors, professionally designed furniture, unique art, and all kinds of lovely and whimsical objects at hundreds of different price points. But along with all that access, we also feel compelled (via our commerce-obsessed culture, media, and advertising) to buy All The Things and then we expect ourselves to display it with flair and panache. With access to All The Things, we've become paralyzed by choice, burdened by a feeling of inadequacy in not having a pretty enough home, and we've lost a lot of our ability to edit, to distinguish wants from needs, and to let things go.

Remember that the glossy images in the architectural magazines are just as airbrushed and photoshopped as the models in fashion and fitness magazines. So use this book to develop your own defenses against the trendsetting home-design "experts," and decorate with confidence, knowing that your home needn't be photo-ready. It just needs to bring a smile to your face when you come home.

Let's make sure your home is working for you, shall we?

FOLLOW THE ADVICE IN THIS BOOK AND YOU CAN ACHIEVE THE FOLLOWING:

- Understand the impact of your space on your life.
- See your home with new eyes.
- Connect your financial, emotional, and physical health to your space.
- Be inspired to let go of what's keeping you from your best life.
- Know how to spend money more wisely on your home.
- Move on from past relationships.
- Take better care of yourself.
- Know what changes you could make to feel prouder of your home.
- Know what changes to make to get your home ready for guests and friends.
- Feel lighter and find it easier to meet weight goals.
- Be more successful in your career ventures.

Where and how you live affects your whole life: your success, your happiness, your health, and your well-being. The place you call home can't help but affect your life. It either launches you forward, vital and full of life, or it holds you back, stagnant. Your exterior life—home, office, even your physical health and appearance—is a manifestation of your internal, emotional life. If you feel you are *less*, if you feel you are *unworthy*, then you'll tend to neglect your home, health, and social life. If the environment around you reinforces those messages of unworthiness, it's easy to spiral deeper into neglect and despair. On the other hand, when you are in a well-tended environment, you take better care of yourself. Your home can help you feel and live more happily. If you do the exercises in this book, you will see change in your life. Really.

I AM GLAD YOU ARE HERE.
If you picked up this book, you probably have an awareness that your home shapes who you are, and that changing your home really can change your life. By the time you are done reading this book, you'll recognize areas where your home could be supporting you better and identify specific areas to make some of those changes. If you are ready for a change, let's get started.

How to Use This Book

THIS ISN'T JUST A READING BOOK. Treat it as a workbook and journal. As you discover answers about what you need in your living space, put the book down, get up, and make some of those changes. Then pick the book back up and venture onward. I encourage you to read through Chapter 1 and complete the exercises, which are universally applicable and set the stage for subsequent chapters.

After you've completed Chapter 1, turn to any chapter that is calling your name and skip any chapters that don't apply to your life. Perhaps refer back to Activity 1, Wheel of Life, and read the chapter that corresponds to the area of your life that you'd like to improve. There is no order in which you have to read the chapters, and there is no magic to doing every last exercise. Each one asks a different question, helping you evaluate your unique situation and discover what you need from your home. With each activity you complete, you'll develop more perspective about your home and be able to see it with new, more objective eyes. This, in turn, will guide you in taking *goal-oriented action in your home.*

Take a moment to gather these tools (they'll come in handy as you work through the chapters):

- Your favorite pen for journaling
- Graph paper for drawing basic floor plans (plain paper will do too)
- Colored pencils or markers
- Your favorite list-making tool (notepad, iPad, cell phone, laptop) for to-dos, to-considers, and to-stop-doings

Feel free to use this book on your own, or involve your family. If you are making big changes, perhaps include your partner or kids in the process and have them complete the activities too. When everyone has a seat at the table, everyone feels respected and heard, and creative solutions often arise.

If you're involving your family, first try to do the activities independently and then compare answers. Let it be an opportunity for discovering differences and brainstorming extraordinary solutions. You can even bring in a third party (an architect, a designer, or a counselor) who is experienced in advising couples if the conversation gets heated. Remember, *your relationships are always more important than the color of the carpet.*

NEST VS. CASTLE: WHEN YOUR SPOUSE JUST DOESN'T GET IT

> **"Sometimes I wonder if men and women really suit each other. Perhaps they should live next door and just visit now and then." —Katharine Hepburn**

In my years of consulting I've seen a scenario play out over and over again: Female clients are eager to make changes in the home but they have a tough time getting their male partners on board with the plan. Many times women assume that men don't care as much about their home, but I have found that to be utterly untrue. While men may not always express interest in the precise wall color or number of throw pillows, I know this for certain: the state of their home deeply affects both women *and* men.

In our culture men are still shouldered with the label of "provider." For a provider, home is a "castle"—tangible evidence of his ability to provide. Women, on the other hand, are still branded with the label "nurturer." For nurturers, the "nest" reflects how well they care for their family. That might explain why some guys desire top-of-the-line electronics (status and providing), and some gals desire attractive décor that will create an inviting, cozy space (nurturing and caring).

Bear in mind that these are vast generalizations, and in your relationship these roles might be flipped, but no matter who is in which role, in my experience this is the cause of too many home remodeling arguments: *you both care, you're just using a completely different language.*

Nests nurture, castles protect.
A home does both, and provides
a refuge for the family.

A nest is meant to nurture friends and family. A castle is meant to protect the family and impress the outsider. But the home has another role too, one that is equally important to both men and women. Home is a "refuge."

We ask three very different things of our homes. We want it to nurture the family, to impress the neighbors, and to serve as a refuge from work and the world. It's quite a challenge to design a space that accomplishes all three. For example, a home might be a great refuge for the spouse who works away from home but it fails to support the person who works from home or is a full-time homemaker because there is no way to "leave work." Just walking through the space means you're staring at your to-do list. This might explain why some people are constantly redecorating; they are in a never-ending struggle to feel relaxed and "at home" in their own house.

Conversely, a house can fail to support those who work outside the home, because it more strongly reflects the tastes and needs of the partner who spends the most time at home. In some homes you can't even tell that a guy lives there. It may be nicely decorated, but it's void of the guy's personality, and it's all off-limits because something might get stained, broken, or misplaced. Guys need a place to recharge too, and that can't happen in a place where they're afraid of breaking something. They retreat into the den, basement, or man cave, the one space where they are "allowed" to relax and be themselves.

The point is, when you uncover what both you *and* your partner need from the house — castle, nest, refuge or, most likely, all three — you'll get a lot further in your discussions about what to change and how much to spend. You'll understand where compromises are okay. And you'll spend a lot less time arguing about the size of the sofa, the color of the carpet, or the price of the countertops.

As Friedrich Nietzsche said, "It is not a lack of love, but a lack of friendship that makes unhappy marriages." Seek to respect your partner's position and truly listen before making changes (or refusing to make changes) to your space. It is their home too.

THE HAPPY STARTS AT HOME PROGRAM

Throughout this book you'll find references to the Happy Starts at Home (HSAH) program. Along with design consultations and interior design services, my design team and I offer an accountability program that helps clients set personal goals for their lives, identify what in the home may be getting in the way of those goals, set identifiable targets for making meaningful change, and provide accountability through check-ins and follow-up calls to help make sure that the ultimate goal is met. In the HSAH program we use many of the tools and exercises that you will find here, but unlike working with a book, we are able to personalize the tools and the pace for each client. Feel free to adapt this book to your needs in the same way: do the exercises that resonate, and make this a useful tool for meeting your goals! Visit happystartsathome.com for other resources, tips, and guidance in the blog, or email me if you need more personal assistance.

Okay, let's get started!

Chapter 1.
Happy Starts with You:
Defining Your Perfect Place

**"Home is any four walls that enclose
the right person." —Helen Rowland**

EVERY HOME IS, AND SHOULD BE, UNIQUE. Your habits, dreams, family, and hobbies are personal to you, and ideally your space reflects and supports your unique lifestyle. There are no rules for setting up your home; it just has to work for you. In this chapter you will zoom out and get perspective on the big picture of your life so that you can zero in on what needs to change. And throughout this book I will show you how to make those changes without losing precious time, money, and sleep.

For starters, it helps to be aware of the effects that our homes have on our lives. Often we make changes guided by what's trending in popular decorating magazines and TV shows. We try to duplicate what is "right" or current, unconsciously trying to keep up with the Joneses without realizing what is motivating our decisions. But the Jones family may like to host parties for forty people every weekend, while you might prefer to spend a lazy Saturday recovering from the workweek. And really, who cares what the Joneses do with *their* place? *Your* home is supposed to make *you* happy and help you reach *your* goals! Comparing your living space to someone else's house or to a magazine spread is like trying to exercise to end up with the body of Audrey Hepburn when, really, you are more of a Marilyn Monroe. It's futile, silly, and pointless. Why not just be a gorgeous Marilyn and let the Audreys be themselves?

YOUR HEART'S DESIRE

**"You must know what you want, to find
what you want." —Lailah Gifty Akita**

Early in my career I worked with a client, Debbie, who was caught in the trap of trying to create the home that *other* people thought she should have. She showed me pictures of the rooms she admired, then asked my advice about what to buy. Based on her visual targets we identified items that would make over her space to resemble the inspiration rooms, and she proceeded to place the orders. But by my next scheduled visit, Debbie had returned everything and had chosen a different design direction for the room. Now, it *can* happen that when you actually get what you were asking for it turns out not to be what you want. Knowing this, I wasn't too worried and we went through the process again. However, when it happened the *third* time, I put on the brakes: it was time to find out what was going on.

It turned out that every time Debbie had made a decision, she'd asked friends and family their opinions about her new décor. Naturally, every-one had offered different opinions, and because she didn't have a strong internal compass guiding her choices, all those opinions left her confused. Debbie lacked the confidence to say what *she* really liked. So before we began the decorating process for the third time, we had a heart-to-heart chat. We explored three important questions: Who did the home need to support? What activities did the home need to support? And how would we know if the work had been successful?

Creating a home that works is about a lot more than the color of the sofa.

The answers to these questions—Whom does your home need to support? What activities happen here? How will you know you've succeeded?—aren't always obvious. At a basic level Debbie's home was a place to eat, sleep, rest, work, and play. That might be factual, but it also doesn't tell us much. In this case the home was for her, yes, but specifically it was for the "grown-up, successful" version of her, trying hard to not need the approval of her family. Debbie and I agreed that her home needed to express her personal identity, and she needed to be comfortable enough to embrace that identity without seeking anyone else's approval. To answer the question "What is my home for?" Debbie expressed that after eight hours or more of caring for other people in her job as a social worker, she longed for a place to recharge so that she could give all that love and energy again the next day. And how would we know her home makeover was a success? If she loved it so much she didn't need her family and friends to love it. It would be a bonus if her family loved it too, but that would be secondary to Debbie liking it on its own merits. Together we set big goals, but with the right mindset and a little help, Debbie discovered they were achievable goals. And very different from just imitating a page in a decorating magazine.

You can see that this kind of work is about more than the color of a sofa. If you take the time to answer the big-picture questions, you'll not only end up with a home you love, but also learn more about yourself and what you need from your career, relationships, and every other part of your life. You'll feel at home not only in your house, but also in your own skin.

Let's begin with a few exercises that will give us a snapshot of how you feel about your home right now, and what you feel is or is not working in your life. We'll touch on what you are trying to achieve in your life, explore areas of your life that are lacking, and identify how your home can help.

> **"Honesty is the first chapter in the book of wisdom."—Thomas Jefferson**

Activity 1. The Wheel of Life: Bridging Your Wellness and Your Home

This exercise will help you discover the areas of your life that are working well and the areas that need support. Then you can laser-focus your energy and plan changes that will make the greatest impact on your life.

The circle has ten sections that correspond with chapters in this book. Look at each section and place a dot on the line marking how satisfied you are with each area of your life. A dot placed at the center of the circle, or close to the center, indicates dissatisfaction; a dot placed on the periphery or edge of the circle indicates ultimate happiness.

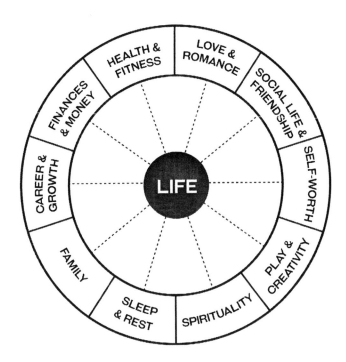

When you have placed a dot on each of the lines, connect the dots. The areas that are full are rich and taken care of, while the flat or dipping areas of the circle show depletion and imbalance. Now you can identify where to spend more time and energy in your home to create balance.

This is the starting point for all the ideas we are about to explore in this book, but your answers will change over time. Mark this page and occasionally revisit your circle. Life is never "done": it is organic and eternally shifting. That means that no matter how much you wish to maintain a balance, the equilibrium will naturally slip. You can use this tool to keep an awareness of what needs attention in your life.

When I work the Happy Starts at Home program with my clients, we begin by taking this snapshot of what is and isn't working in their lives. We use their circle to define the intention behind making changes. Action is best taken when there is intent behind it. Intent keeps momentum going and allows for easier decision making.

Let's say your intent is to "be more fit" and you want your house to support you in that effort. As you sort through your workout clothes, unearth the workout equipment, and create a place to support your mission of getting fit, you'll have clarity and intention behind these changes and decisions. You'll know what kind of time and money to spend because you'll know what it is worth to you to get fit. On the other hand, if you just dive into your mission without having a compelling "why" beyond feeling like you "should," you'll lose steam before you've even uncovered the treadmill. You'll have failed to create an exercise environment that encourages you to use it, and you'll have "proven" to yourself that you can't succeed.

As you completed Activity 1, the Wheel of Life, did you find any surprises? Did you discover unexpected areas in which you felt satisfied? Perhaps an area being neglected that you hadn't thought about in a while? Many times we "kind of" know the dissatisfied aspects of our lives, but putting it on paper helps us more honestly assess ourselves and our situations.

Slices of Life Recap

Areas that are full and rich right now:	Areas that are lacking and need attention:
_____	_____
_____	_____
_____	_____
_____	_____
_____	_____

Activity 2. Quiz: How Happy Is Your Home?
This quiz will help you think through your level of contentment at home. Answer each question with a rating of 1 to 5, 1 being least like you and 5 being most like you.

1 = Not at all true, never true, or not at all like me
2 = Not as true as I'd like, rarely true
3 = Sometimes true, half the time true
4 = More often than not true, frequently like me
5 = Absolutely true, always like me, or all the time

Tally the results to rate your level of satisfaction and determine if your house is supporting or sabotaging you.

Quiz: How Happy Is My Home?

When I walk up to my entry door, I start to feel more relaxed.	1 2 3 4 5
I find it easy to cook healthy meals at home.	1 2 3 4 5
I sleep soundly through the night in my bedroom.	1 2 3 4 5
I never apologize for my home when someone comes over.	1 2 3 4 5
There are no doors I keep closed to hide the clutter.	1 2 3 4 5
Every room in my home is well used by at least one person.	1 2 3 4 5
Every person has at least one room that reflects their personality.	1 2 3 4 5
I never have trouble finding what I need in my home.	1 2 3 4 5
I have plenty of storage space for my belongings.	1 2 3 4 5
Everything is in good repair in my home.	1 2 3 4 5
I have good lighting for all my tasks in every room.	1 2 3 4 5
My home easily accommodates my hobbies and activities.	1 2 3 4 5
Nothing in my home makes me feel guilty or sad.	1 2 3 4 5
Nothing in my home makes me feel frustrated.	1 2 3 4 5
Nothing in my home nags at me "to do."	1 2 3 4 5
I feel at home in my home.	1 2 3 4 5
It is easy for me to pick up and clean my home.	1 2 3 4 5
I have a comfortable place for guests.	1 2 3 4 5
My home makes me feel comfortable and at ease.	1 2 3 4 5
My home reflects my values.	1 2 3 4 5

Tally up your score.   _____

0–40 points. Struggling: Your space actively weighs you down. You may feel frustrated, and you may not feel at home in your house. When you look around you see bad decisions, or your past, or someone else's past. Maybe you feel a sense of failure or maybe the place is just not up to the standards you have set for yourself. You are likely tired of this feeling. You just want to feel calm, peaceful, and proud of your home, but you aren't sure that is possible. You may feel stuck or helpless. Maybe you've set goals to finish a room or get organized, but you're always too busy or too overwhelmed to get very far. You would love a solution, but you don't know where to start.

What you need: A shift in energy. A vision that will encourage you, empower you, and guide you out of this rut. An understanding that your situation is temporary and changeable. Actionable, small steps that fit into your busy life and create a sense of change and accomplishment. Proof that you are not alone; there is nothing wrong with you; you are not a failure; and you can feel calm, peaceful, and empowered about your home and your life.

41–75 points. Striving: Your space has some pluses and some minuses. There is room for improvement, but you are hopeful. Your home feels safe and secure but could feel a bit more welcoming, cozy, and comfortable. You know that you have a good life, but you're never quite relaxed. You are ready to fully love your home and have it work for you instead of you working for it.

What you need: Clarity around what is working and what can be done to bring you to a more complete place. An action plan to help you finish the "incompletes" in your home and prioritize projects so you get the biggest impact for your effort. Small but focused steps to make sure your surroundings are working for you and ensuring your success rather than sabotaging all your hard work.

76–100 points. Succeeding and supporting: Congratulations! Your home is helping you succeed. You've done the work to create a space that supports you. You regularly donate items that have outlived their purpose, and you don't hesitate to buy things that will bring an element of joy or functionality to your home, because you sense when your home needs a change.

What you need: More of the same: keep it up! Occasional freshening up as your life shifts. Continued good habits that will make it easier to keep an ear out for when your home is asking for an update.

Now that we have that snapshot of your life, let's ask some questions about your home.

"WHO" IS YOUR HOME?

"A home should be a shelter for the soul as well as the body." —Samuel Mockbee

Your home is so much more than just an impersonal roof over your head. In fact, the personality of your home "lives with you" and influences you as much as the actual people and pets that share your space. That means it's important to figure out just "who" it is you are living with. Unfortunately, many of us are living with bullies that keep us in a state of stress and prevent us from living an abundant life.

It's much like the way financial coach Morgana Rae personifies money. Rae says that during her early financial struggles, Money was like a big, dirty, scary biker guy who caused fights at parties, the kind of person she would rather avoid than confront. Every time she had to interact with Money, she had to deal with This Guy. Like Rae, we all have a relationship with money, and if you are having trouble with your finances, giving money a name and character identity can be a helpful way to figure out what is troubling you.

The home is the same way. How would you answer the question, "Who are you living with?" If your home were a *person* that woke up next to you every day, stood in the kitchen each morning when you poured your first cup of coffee, and waited at the front door when you arrived, who would it be? For me, my home is like a best friend who waits for me at the front door with cookies and flowers, and who greets me in the kitchen with a cheery "Good morning." Nice, eh?

It wasn't always that way. After my divorce, my home was more like Eeyore, the somber gray donkey in *Winnie the Pooh* with a droopy, hopeless, defeated outlook and a tendency to remind me of the bad decisions I'd made. After a few months of living with *that* person I'd finally had enough. I refused to hear another word against me; I refused to keep living in my past. I wanted my home to remind me I had a bright, exciting, successful future. It was time to toss out Eeyore and invite a new friend into my home. So I repainted the walls, sold most of my furniture, and bought all "new" furniture on Craigslist. Voilà! I was living in a new home, with a new story, and with a new "friend" who could support and encourage me, and help me look toward my future with enthusiasm instead of looking at my past with regret.

That was my experience, the story of my home. Now it's time to identify *your* home's personality. If you can give it a name, even better, because the more you're able to personify the character of your home, the more easily you'll figure out what needs to change. What does your home say to you? How does it make you feel? Describe your home as if it were a person that you know.

> *Example:* Eeyore makes me feel stupid. He makes me feel like I made *big mistakes and he won't let me forget it. Ever. He makes me feel like I am not good enough to do anything lucrative, like I should go back to being an admin assistant at my old financial firm. Sure, I hated it, but I was decent at it. He won't let me let go of the past, and he refuses to let me have a future. According to him, all I am good for is . . . nothing.*

Whew! Writing something like that can be really scary. I mean, was I really living with someone that cruel? Would I have ever let my best friend live with a real person like that? *No!* Then why was *I* living with a "person" like that?

Okay, take a deep breath: now it's your turn. What does your home say to you, and how does it make you feel?

Activity 3. If My House Were a Person
To help you frame the conversation, here are some words that have commonly come up for my clients as they have worked through this exercise.

(Note: Since most of my clients come to me in a time of lack or stuck-ness, you'll notice these are mostly negative words. But if you are in a positive place, share those words and feelings freely!)

unwelcome	shaming	messy	pessimistic
nosy	detached	cold	dirty
stressful	crowding	confused	uncommitted
self-interested	possessive	disconnected	too helpful
pressuring	unemotional	demanding	misguided
busy	loud	belittling	embarrassing
aloof	judging	better than me	out of control

My house is:

_____

_____

_____

_____

_____

How'd that go? Were you surprised by whom you've been living with? Maybe your house is like a nagging sister who thinks you never do enough, or a bossy friend who suggests you're lazy, or a well-meaning mother who knows what's "best for you." The only question left is, "Do I really want to live with *that* person?"

Now for the fun part. With whom do you *want* to live?

When I made over my house after my divorce, I didn't really make a plan at first. I only knew I refused to go on the way that I'd been living. I needed a change, and in my desperation I didn't care what the change looked like so long as it looked different. At first this resulted in a very unfortunate choice of nearly black paint on my ceiling and a screaming turquoise accent wall in a lime-green room. My room went from "depressed" to "angry"—appropriate, I suppose, since I was practically drowning in anger and frustration and didn't have a guide helping me to see past those emotions.

It was just paint, so it didn't matter too much. It got me past feeling stuck. And just by getting unstuck I found some perspective and the ability to take a longer view of where my life was headed. I realized I needed to let myself heal. A couple of weeks later, I painted over the angry-colored walls in a soft shade of pink that created a feminine cocoon where I could be at peace before I headed back out into the scary world of dating and relationships.

I'd like to spare you the "angry wall" phase if I can, but know that if you need to create that emotional place for yourself, *it's okay.* Just try to do it with inexpensive changes: avoid making big, costly changes like tile, flooring, and cabinets during times of big transition in your life.

So, whom *do* you want to live with? After I painted my walls soft shell pink, this is how I would have described my house:

> *She makes me feel calm and feminine. When I am with my home I feel like I have a purpose in this life. That purpose isn't clear to me yet, but*

my home gives me a space where it is okay not to know yet and to trust that the answers will come. My home welcomes my new friends and they love to be here, which means that I spend more time with them, drinking my favorite Pinot Grigio and laughing. I feel like things are possible, and my home whispers encouragement. She doesn't rush me to make decisions; she just holds me as I heal.

What would you like to be able to say about your home? Who would you choose as a roommate? Write this next paragraph, if you can, as if you are already living in that place:

When it best supports me, my home is like this:

_____

_____

_____

_____

_____

_____

The future you want *is* possible. You *can* come home to a house that makes you happy and that sends you out into the world full of courage, joy, and love. To make way for your wonderful new life, it helps to clear out some of the old stuff. After all, you can't make fresh, delicious cookies with old, stale ingredients.

> **"Life can only be understood backwards;
> but it must be lived forwards."**
> **—Søren Kierkegaard**

Before you think about your future, and are able to let go of the past and live in the moment, it's helpful to acknowledge where you came from and to see the path that brought you here.

Activity 4. Past, Present, Future

Take a moment to look back—physically, emotionally, financially, relationally, and spiritually. Describe the emotional state of your past, of your present, and of your desired future.

The Past: Childhood

In each blank, write up to three adjectives that describe how you lived as a child:

My health was _____

My playtime was _____

Our finances were _____

My faith was _____

I slept _____

I studied _____

My friends were _____

I imagined _____

I felt _____

My parents were _____

The Present

In each blank, write up to three adjectives that describe how you feel during this present chapter of your life:

My health is _____

My playtime is _____

My finances are _____

My faith is _____

I sleep _____

I learn _____

My friends are _____

When I daydream I _____

I feel _____

Love is _____

The Future

In each blank, write up to three adjectives that describe how you want to feel during this next chapter in your life:

My health will be _____

My playtime will be _____

My finances will be _____

My faith will be _____

I will sleep _____

I will learn _____

My friends will be _____

When I daydream I _____

I will feel _____

Love will be _____

By completing this past, present, and future assessment, you name the places you've been, you recognize the place where you are now, and you visualize the place you'd like to be.

To move forward, each of us must step on the stones that make up the path of our lives. Some of the stones are sharp, others slippery; with luck most are solid and steady. Regardless, that path, each step, makes us what we are. If we learn from each step, we can walk confidently into our future. Here you have taken a moment to honor the path that led you here, understood just where it is you've ended up, and defined a vision for where you want to be. Hold on to that vision as you make choices for your home.

Activity 5. Identifying Priorities

A clear and focused vision makes it possible to spend your money and time wisely as you work toward your desired outcome. We've established that your home is a tool for helping you realize your dreams and, as with any tool, in order to use it well it's good to know what you wish to build. With that in mind, let's get even clearer about your intentions and priorities. This exercise includes two columns so that two people can answer: if you live with a partner, a spouse, an adult child, or a housemate, it is important that you create space for *both* of your needs to be fulfilled. *Use this exercise to find common ground, not to find fault with the other person's wishes or desires.* Number your priorities from one (most important) to ten (least important).

My current priorities for my home include:

Person 1	Person 2	
_____	_____	To start my life from scratch
_____	_____	To put down roots
_____	_____	To live near my family or in-laws

_____	_____	To give me a project or indulge an interest or hobby
_____	_____	To allow my relationships to develop and mature
_____	_____	To start a family
_____	_____	To bring up my children
_____	_____	To live near work
_____	_____	To enjoy my retirement
_____	_____	Other _____

Once you complete the activity, look at your top three priorities. Does your home meet those needs? Also, if applicable, evaluate how your needs and your partner's needs complement or compete with each other, and look for common ground.

The top three things I need from my home right now are:

_____

_____

_____

The changes I'd like to make in my home to support my needs are:

_____

_____

_____

_____

_____

_____

TAKE AN INVENTORY

> **"Some people believe holding on and hanging in there are signs of great strength. However, there are times when it takes much more strength to know when to let go and then do it." —Ann Landers**

What is all that stuff in your home, anyway? In the modern age we tend to collect, accumulate, accept, buy, and gather. Rarely do we release, decrease, and declutter. The result is as if I told you that you could buy as many new clothes as you wanted, but *you could never, ever take off anything you'd already purchased.* In just one or two shopping trips you'd be wearing so much clothing that it would be hard to walk. You'd feel hot and irritable, and be unable to do anything well. The accumulation in our homes can be every bit as much of a burden!

Every item rents a space in your heart and in your brain. If there is too much stuff, then you have little room for new fun, new love, or new anything. So let's take a look at what is really in your home. Where did all that furniture, décor, and stuff come from? Why is it in your life, and what purpose does it serve? What feelings are associated with each object?

It's time to inventory all that stuff. Now, there is no way we can catalog every item in your home. That would take forever and it wouldn't be helpful. There is such a thing as too much information. Instead, let's do a baker's dozen mini-inventory of your home.

Activity 6. The Happy Starts at Home Assessment

I'd like to show you an efficient way to inventory your stuff in three stages. First, take an Honest Inventory of what is in your home. Second, go on an Emotional Scavenger Hunt to seek out the good and bad feelings living in your home. Both of these are meant to give you a chance to see your home with new eyes. Third, jot some notes in the Home Exploration Journal, taking time to reflect on where you are, mentally and emotionally, with your home right now and what you want from it when you are finished with this process.

HSAH ASSESSMENT PART 1: AN HONEST INVENTORY

First, choose a room and list a dozen items in that space. Try to list a couple of big furniture pieces, a couple of accessories or artsy pieces, maybe some gifts, maybe some semi-permanent features like paint colors or light fixtures.

Next to each one of your twelve items, write the first feeling that comes to mind when you think of it. Common words can include: nostalgic, poor, happy, rich, sad, frustrated, loved, annoyed, and neutral. (Be careful using neutral. Does that object really have *zero* emotion attached to it?)

Next, record when you last used the item. "Used" can mean sat on, shared, enjoyed, or worn.

Now identify who bought or chose each item. Was it you? Your spouse? Ex-spouse? Friend? Mother? Sister? The home's previous owner?

Finally, note *why* it was purchased. Was it to solve a specific problem? To make someone else happy? Because you loved it?

Item: _____   Emotion: _____   Last used: _____
Bought/chosen by: _____   Reason for it: _____

Item: _____   Emotion: _____   Last used: _____
Bought/chosen by: _____   Reason for it: _____

Item: _____   Emotion: _____   Last used: _____
Bought/chosen by: _____   Reason for it: _____

Item: _____   Emotion: _____   Last used: _____
Bought/chosen by: _____   Reason for it: _____

Item: _____   Emotion: _____   Last used: _____
Bought/chosen by: _____   Reason for it: _____

Item: _____   Emotion: _____   Last used: _____
Bought/chosen by: _____   Reason for it: _____

Item: _____   Emotion: _____   Last used: _____
Bought/chosen by: _____   Reason for it: _____

Item: _____   Emotion: _____   Last used: _____
Bought/chosen by: _____   Reason for it: _____

Item: _____   Emotion: _____   Last used: _____
Bought/chosen by: _____   Reason for it: _____

Item: _____   Emotion: _____   Last used: _____
Bought/chosen by: _____   Reason for it: _____

Item: _____   Emotion: _____   Last used: _____
Bought/chosen by: _____   Reason for it: _____

Item: _____   Emotion: _____   Last used: _____
Bought/chosen by: _____   Reason for it: _____

Review your list. Do any themes emerge? Did you buy stuff that you loved at the time but now it makes you feel guilty? Do you have stuff that someone else likes but it only makes you feel frustrated? There is no judgment here, just an opportunity for you to become more aware of your belongings.

HSAH ASSESSMENT PART 2: EMOTIONAL SCAVENGER HUNT
Now we are going to do this in reverse, rather like a scavenger hunt. First, list five feelings that you *want* to get from your home (like warmth, hope, and acceptance) and five feelings you do *not* want from your home (like pain, guilt, and shame).

Take the list and find five objects that evoke each of the positive feelings. For each item, identify the good feeling and who brought that item into your home.

Next, find five objects that elicit each of the negative emotions. For each item, identify who brought that item into your home and ask yourself why you keep that item in your life.

Good feeling	Item	Who bought/chose it	Last enjoyed

Bad feeling	Item	Who bought/chose it	Why I keep it

With your list in hand, dig a little more deeply. First, from the good-feelings list, where did most of those items come from? Do you use them? Do you keep them where you can see them, or are they hidden by other stuff?

Take a moment to journal your thoughts:

_____

_____

_____

_____

Now look at the bad feelings list. What makes you keep the things that cause you pain? Is it unawareness of the feelings held in that object? Guilt for the money you spent? Fear that you won't find anything better? Shame for making a bad decision? How is holding on making you feel? Can you let go now?

Take a moment to journal your thoughts:

_____

_____

_____

_____

_____

_____

Once you complete Parts 1 and 2, you will begin to recognize patterns in your home that may have been invisible before. It is time to see your home as if you'd never been there before.

HSAH ASSESSMENT PART 3: HOME EXPLORATION JOURNAL

This third inventory stage will help you evaluate both the assets and liabilities in your home. Read and think about the following questions and journal your answers below. (If you are eager to move forward it is okay to skip ahead to the next chapter and come back to your Home Exploration Journal later.)

- How is my home supporting me right now?
- How is my home sabotaging me right now?
- What goals do I have in the next six months that my home needs to support? How about the next year? Three years?

_____

_____

_____

_____

_____

_____

- How do I feel about my home when people come over?
- How do I wish to feel when people come over?
- What is the main obstacle getting in the way of how I want to feel when people come over?

_____

_____

_____

_____

_____

_____

- Is everything in my home either beautiful or useful?
- What in my home is neither beautiful nor useful? Why is it in my home? If it were gone, what would change?

_____

_____

_____

_____

_____

_____

- What am I holding on to in my space that creates unhappiness? Why am I holding on to it?
- What do I want to create space for in my home and in my life? What would need to go for me to have that?

_____

_____

_____

_____

_____

_____

When you answer these questions honestly, you'll gain a strong sense of what needs to shift in your home as you move forward.

TO SUM UP

You're probably catching on to the point: when you are thinking about updating your home, it's not as simple as picking a color. As Marni Jameson writes in *The House Always Wins*, "Many people wrongly approach decorating by first focusing on a color scheme. But the first question to ask is more basic. What are you planning to do in your home? By defining your purpose . . . you will define your lifestyle. In great design, function comes first, form second." With my clients, I describe this as choosing your vacation destination (Sunny Florida? Wild Alaska?) and *then* deciding what to pack. It's no good asking what kind of jacket to bring if you haven't determined where you are going, and it's equally pointless to ask what color you should paint your walls, whether or not you need a lamp in the corner, or what model fridge to buy without first determining how you want to live in your space. Before we even talk about décor, I ask my clients, "Well, how do you use (or wish to use) the space?"

Choosing a paint color for your room before looking at the big picture of your home is like packing your suitcase before you decide where you are vacationing.

It's okay to meet some resistance as you think about making changes. As behavior science writer Winifred Gallagher notes, when we start to consider repositioning the living room furniture, or try to convince our family to hang their coats in the closet instead of dumping them on a chair, we find that "what started out as '*a* way' has somehow turned into '*the* way,' becoming so entrenched that otherwise competent people are reduced to paying a professional to find a better spot for the piano."

Gallagher adds that once we have that set way of doing things, these patterns "close our minds to better options and incline us toward knee-jerk reactions." Because we do get stuck when we try to look at our own situations, you may find that you do, in fact, need some outside help to get unstuck, just like you would if your car slid into a ditch. You wouldn't think twice about calling a tow truck because you know it would be silly to try to yank it out of the ditch with your own two hands. It is important and wise to ask for help when you need it.

By doing the exercises in this chapter you've already made great strides toward understanding what is and isn't working in your home and in your life. You've started assessing the contents of your home: how it all got there, why it has stayed, and how it affects you. Assuming you want a change, it's now time to shake things up and shift your reality. At times it will be tough, and sometimes it'll feel like two steps back and one step forward. But don't worry: as psychobiologist Myron Hofer, MD, says, "We find confusion hard to tolerate, but it allows us to see things the way they really are."

It's time to look at the specific areas of your life from the Wheel of Life activity that need support, and figure out how your home can help you feel fulfilled in those areas. I promise you'll see that changes are possible, find the courage to shake things up, and create the happy home—and life—you've always wanted.

Chapter 2.
Happy and Financially Fit:
Establishing an Abundant Life

"Every time you spend money you cast a
vote for the kind of world you want."
—Anna Lappé

WHY START WITH MONEY? According to the American Psychological Association and the American Institute of Stress, 76 percent of Americans name money as the number one factor that affects their stress level. If three out of four people find money to be the most stressful relationship in their lives, it seems like a good place to start when talking about changing our lives in order to be happier.

What does your home have to do with improving your relationship with money? Everything. Let's look at three ways your home and your wealth are interconnected.

First, your home may be out of alignment with your actual income or wealth. This happens when the stuff in your home makes you feel poor and broke, when in fact you are financially stable. If this is the case, your home may be a barrier between you and great success in your health, relationships, and general happiness.

Let's refer to this scenario as "Money without a Life." To the outside world, you look like you have it made. You may live in a beautiful home, but inside the walls of your home you are not at peace. Nothing in your home says that you are successful or capable. At best, it feels uninspiring. At worst it looks and feels like a lazy, incompetent, scattered person lives there. It embarrasses you because you're successful in so many ways. Why doesn't your home feel good? If you feel this way, you are not alone. Many of my clients have successful careers but haven't experienced that success in their homes and relationships yet.

On the other hand, maybe you are not currently blessed with financial abundance. Perhaps your home is stuffed with stuff, but you feel a distinct lack of plentitude. You may feel that no matter how hard you work, you struggle to make ends meet. At the same time, you find your home overwhelming. Something always needs doing or fixing, and everything you buy to improve the space seems to fall short. Despite your efforts, your space is full but unsatisfying.

Let's call this second scenario "Under-abundance." Your financial situation is unsteady, and the balance between income and bills always feels precarious. Your home is full, but your life is anything but abundant. It feels like there is both too much and not enough all at the same time. To make matters worse, your resources are stretched so tightly that you don't feel like you can afford to make changes. If this is you, you are also not alone. In our culture it is easy to feel both overstretched *and* overstuffed.

It can feel like there is both too much and not enough all at the same time.

It is also possible that rather than feeling out of step with the money you have, or struggling with the money you don't have, you actually feel disconnected from the objects in your life. Your home may be bare or it may be beautiful, but either way you didn't have much to do with creating it. Perhaps you moved into your new spouse's home. Or perhaps you've moved so many times that you've given up decorating. Or maybe you are in a relationship with someone with a demanding personality and you've abdicated decision-making to your partner. If you're disinterested in your home, chances are you're similarly disengaged from your financial planning too.

Let's call this third scenario "Powerlessness." You don't really have too much or too little money, but you have a difficult relationship with money and have trouble asking for what you need. You hate starting conversations about money with your spouse, your boss, or your employees. Money is a topic you would rather just avoid. You accept what is handed to you; it may be all you feel you are worth. Somehow you have come to a place in your life where you let others make decisions for you. The result is that you can blame others for a bad outcome, but it also means that you are not really in charge of your home or your life. If you feel this way, I understand. I found myself in this position at one time in my own life.

Decision-making, and taking responsibility for outcomes, is like a muscle: it can grow weak or grow strong, depending on use. So how about you? When it comes to money, have you taken responsibility and made decisions you're proud of? See if you recognize yourself in any of the following three scenarios.

MONEY SCENARIO 1: MONEY WITHOUT A LIFE

> **"I believe that being successful means having a balance of success stories across the many areas of your life. You can't truly be considered successful in your business life if your home life is in shambles."**
> **—Zig Ziglar**

If you are living out the first scenario, you are financially flush but you haven't achieved the happiness you thought would come with that monetary success. You may have a great job, a position of power, and a life you're generally proud of, but you kind of dread coming home. There is a huge disconnect between what you wake up to each day and what you are trying to achieve in your life. This can work for a while, but it takes a toll, and if you are building a powerful career and living an energetic life, you need to reserve your energy and make sure every resource you have supports and recharges you as you conquer the world. I had a client in just this situation.

Successful lawyer at work, college kid at home

My client Marissa, a successful lawyer in her late thirties, lived in an upscale apartment with a gorgeous water view, but it was furnished like an undergrad's dorm room. Since the day Marissa moved in, she'd looked forward to buying a home and getting married; as a result she'd treated the apartment as a temporary crash pad. Marissa didn't want to bother investing her precious time, love, or money into a place she planned to leave. Somehow, though, five years had passed and she still lived as if she'd just moved in. Marissa grew tired of that disconnect and of feeling embarrassed to invite people over.

The changes we made to Marissa's apartment were subtle—no paint, no remodeling—and inexpensive: we shopped online and at Ikea and focused on creating a warm, elegant, and inviting space, designing it all around her grandmother's fabulous midcentury chair. The results? At first, Marissa just reveled in the newfound joy of coming home to a place that felt like her. Then, by feeling more at home, more aligned in her life, big changes started happening. Within a year Marissa met and married the man of her dreams and bought the house she'd always wanted. When we worked together again, now fitting the furniture we'd chosen into her new home, she just glowed. Marissa had found her home, in more ways than one.

Young, free, and single: Dashing and daring, or depressed and dateless?

I worked with another client, Derek, in a similar predicament. This young, attractive, and single man ran his own business, earned his PhD, and owned a beautiful, modern minimalist house. Even with all that success, he lived like a bachelor in an almost cartoonish way: mattress on the floor, bedsheet tacked over the window as a curtain. The place was spare, cold, and unfriendly—the opposite of this vibrant guy. To make matters worse, he had trouble sleeping at night. He didn't want to live like this. He really wanted a "cocoon," a place that felt comfortable, restful, and fun for his friends.

After we completed the changes in his home, he experienced immediate (and, quite literally, overnight) success. The day after we finished his bedroom, complete with velvet ripple-fold drapes that enclosed his king-size bed, Derek slept not only through the night but also right through the start of our meeting the next morning. While I might have preferred not to stand at his door for fifteen minutes, ringing the bell, knocking, calling his cell, I couldn't help but smile at this beautiful sign of a successful project! After the makeover Derek started throwing home parties, and it became a natural place for him to entertain his friends and to recharge before he went out each day to conquer the world.

What does all this have to do with money? Both Marissa and Derek had achieved monetary success and felt satisfied in their work. But the dissonance between their successful careers and their uninviting homes prevented them from feeling content with their home, social, and romantic lives. They were holding it together, *but once their houses felt like homes they didn't need to "hold it together."* Marissa's and Derek's home makeovers made it possible for them to build on their successes and get even more out of life. Investing time and money turned out to be a great choice for both of these clients with a fantastic return on their investments.

No matter what our level of wealth, we can't help but be influenced by our environment. Why do you think advertising works so well? We take in messages and apply them to our lives. What we perceive, we believe. In the end, a dripping faucet or a mattress on the floor will make you feel broke no matter how much money you make. If you tend to your space and make the changes needed to reflect your hard work and your dreams, each day you'll feel more relaxed and confident, and in turn discover greater success in your work, love, and health. When you already feel great about your career, feeling great at home is the last piece of the puzzle: fit in that piece, and you can create a complete picture.

MONEY SCENARIO 2: UNDER-ABUNDANCE

> **"Abundance is not something we
> acquire. It is something we tune into."**
> **—Wayne Dyer**

If you are like my clients Marissa and Derek in Scenario 1, congratulations! You already have a full and abundant life; now your job is to make sure that your heart and home are in alignment. But, if you are like many people, you may be struggling to make ends meet. Your home may be full, even stuffed, to the brim, but your life is anything but abundant. It may feel like there is both too much and not enough all at the same time.

Money coach and author Mikelann Valterra says that with each purchase we make we are really asking, "Am I perfect yet?" or "Can you love me now?" or "Am I good enough yet?" When we see lifestyle images of gorgeous, happy people sitting on $10,000 Ralph Lauren sofas and cooking in their professional-style kitchens worthy of Tom Douglas, we want in on that world. It's not that we want the couch, really, it's that we want the lifestyle it promises—one where we are beautiful, loved, and free from worry. Over and over we are told through words and pictures that all it takes to access that world is a simple purchase! Valterra says that women, in particular, tend to purchase things that promise to make life better for their families. We see these messages and think, either consciously or unconsciously, "If a kitchen remodel is what it will take to create that Rockwell lifestyle, we'd better do it before the kids get too much older!"

We spend because we are looking for something. We buy because of the promise of a happier life.

So we spend because we are seeking a solution. We buy new homes, new kitchens, new organizing systems, new clothes, all in an attempt to create a better life. We go on vacation, send the kids to music camp, eat dinner out— always chasing happiness. Sometimes we end up happier, sometimes we don't. But one thing is certain: when we overspend, we end up less happy.

I regularly help people remodel their homes and create chef-worthy kitchens and spa-like baths, and if it is in your budget and aligns with your goals and values, I say go for it. The problem comes when you don't take the time to figure out the best value for your money and when you spend money on things that don't solve the real problem. Any time you are doing something because you feel you "should," a big red flag should go up in your brain. Stop and ask, "Why? *Why should I?*" "Should" is rarely, if ever, a good enough reason.

Have you ever decided you "should" get organized? Did you go out and buy adorable color-coded bins and labels, and then find yourself so over-whelmed that instead of getting organized, you shoved the new bins and labels into the spare room with all the kids' old toys, magazines, and things you meant to return—along with all the rest of the Stuff? That good intention to get organized somehow moved you one step *further* away from having that charming guest room or dedicated office space. Now you just own a bigger pile of stuff, and it weighs you down even more.

Don't get me wrong: money is an important tool for getting the things we need to survive and to thrive. Spending can be important, but spending without focus just drains your resources, fails to get you closer to happiness, and increases stress by building up both piles of stuff and piles of debt. In *The Secret*, James Ray says that "life is meant to be abundant in all areas." It's true, but what does "abundant" mean? There is an important relationship between quality and abundance—*a bunch of garbage in our lives does not equal abundance*.

Living with abundance is learning how to recognize plenty and how to spend wisely. Sometimes a kitchen remodel is in order. Sometimes you really can use that amazing organizing system. But oftentimes you really need to let things go and create new spending habits in order to create a happier home and a happier relationship with money. In order to do that, we have to know where all the money is going, and where all the stuff is coming from.

So, where *does* all that stuff come from? It comes from three main sources: Stuff is bought and kept out of *fear*. Stuff is collected and kept out of *love*. And stuff is kept and multiplied out of *habit*.

WE KEEP STUFF OUT OF FEAR

> **"Courage is not the absence of fear, but rather the judgment that something else is more important than fear."**
> **—Ambrose Hollingsworth Redmoon**

Sometimes we keep stuff because we fear nothing better will come along. Sometimes we dread the unknown and feel more comfortable with our unhappy but familiar lives. Sometimes we think we are being "prepared." Being *prepared* is a special trap we fall into, because it sounds so noble. We have a responsibility to our families to be ready for anything. We carry eight different snacks and five different toys in the baby bag just to be ready to meet Junior's whim. We save boxes for shoes, appliances, electronics—just about anything!—in case we need to return them, or pack up and move someday, or mail a gift. We stockpile food from Costco so we are ready for the zombie apocalypse.

By keeping this stuff in my house, what fear am I holding on to?

Your preparedness might be well intended, but be careful. As Maxwell Gillingham-Ryan writes in *Apartment Therapy*, "'Being prepared' can sometimes be a euphemism for being scared to let go. How much we carry—whether it is on our bicycle, in our bag, or in our home—is often directly related to how little we trust in life to guide us well, and in others to help us out in a pinch."

Stacy Erickson, owner of Home Key Organization, says she hears the excuses all the time. As she sorts through piles with her clients, she regularly hears "I might need that later" or "It could be good for a craft project for the kids." Erickson says, "Saving stuff doesn't save you either time or money. The cost of organizing it, storing it, looking for it . . . it all adds up to more than the cost of rebuying it if you had to (which, let's admit, is probably unlikely). It's just fear making you hold on."

When you take a leap and start letting things go from your home, you'll open the door to trust and opportunity. That in turn can help you learn to see life with abundant eyes and worry less about money. So ask yourself, "By keeping this stuff in my house, what fear am I holding on to?"

WE KEEP STUFF OUT OF LOVE

> **"Letting go means to come to the realization that some people are a part of your history, but not a part of your destiny."**
> **—Steve Maraboli**

Love. It's a great excuse for holding on. What does love-clutter look like? It looks like the two sets of antique china that never get used. It looks like the two dozen boxes of photographs and letters that you always meant to scrapbook. It looks like a garage full of stuff the kids left behind when they moved out. Or like the closet full of gifts you meant, but forgot, to give, or the gifts someone gave you that you will never use but that you feel horrible about giving away. It's also in the piles and piles of art pages from elementary school for the kid who's now learning to drive, and in the antique hutch that your sister wants you to keep because it belonged to Great Aunt Betty.

Although your impulse to keep these things may start with love, the stuff can still become a burden. Here are three ways to deal with heirlooms, memorabilia, and other stuff that could be categorized as "special."

If your sister hadn't guilted you into keeping Great Aunt Betty's hutch, would you keep it in your home?

First, evaluate if you are keeping the stuff out of love or guilt. If your sister hadn't guilted you into keeping Great Aunt Betty's hutch, would you keep it in your home? If the answer is no, then perhaps it belongs in your sister's home. If your sister doesn't value the hutch enough to store it in her own house, perhaps it could be given to someone who would really love it. (The excuse "But she's renting—someday she'll take it!" doesn't always hold water. Have an honest conversation with yourself, or her, about when it has simply been long enough.)

Second, evaluate if you are keeping the stuff out of nostalgia. Stacks of art created by your child are precious but can also become a burden. Sometimes keeping one or two pieces is all you need to bring back the memories of that special time. It is natural for you, as a parent, to want to hold on to those years, but part of being a good parent is letting your children grow and change, and an important piece of that process is letting go. Your kids can learn this lesson too, and you can teach by doing. The earlier you start the habit of keeping only one or two memory pieces, the easier and more "normal" it will become, and both you and your kids will learn to edit and separate what is precious from what is superfluous.

Third, be aware that someday *someone* will have to go through all that stuff. If you've lost a parent you probably know how overwhelming it is to sort through eighty years of someone's history and figure out what to keep and what to dump. Cutting through some of that clutter now is not only a kindness to yourself, it relieves a huge burden for those who come after. No matter what age you are, start today so that no one else has to sort through twelve boxes of letters and photographs and two decades of *National Geographic* magazines.

Always keep what brings you true joy, but if the things you *claim* bring you true joy are stuffed in boxes mildewing in the garage, or are piled so deep on the mantle that you can't even see them, reconsider whether those objects really matter. Is the stuff serving you and being honored, or is it just creating a burden for you and those to follow you?

WE KEEP STUFF OUT OF HABIT

> **"You will find that it is necessary to let things go; simply for the reason that they are heavy. So let them go, let go of them. I tie no weights to my ankles."**
> **—C. JoyBell C.**

It's amazing what happens in our lives just out of habit. One of my clients had saved cereal box tops for her kid's school program. She continued saving box tops for twelve years, long after the kid had graduated from college. There were bags of box tops stuffed in her garage!

Cereal box tops, packing boxes, grocery bags, little gift bags, all the little bits of possibly useful stuff that at one time seemed so practical. You keep plastic grocery bags to clean the litter box, but you no longer have a cat? What? Well, you say, you might get a cat again. Okay, when you do, you can start saving the bags again.

You used to ship care packages to your son in college? Now he lives in the next town and you just bring goodies over for the grandkids? Maybe you don't need forty-two packing boxes. Maybe someone else can use them.

Habits are not easily broken, and part of you will resist, protesting that those boxes, bags, containers—you name it—could be really useful some-day. Now's the time to give that habitualized part of you a stern talking-to. Remember that you are moving on, life has changed, and holding on to all that stuff is a burden, not a blessing. And when you do need a bunch of packing boxes, the universe will provide. Have enough faith to be generous now.

"If you rent a storage facility to store your excess belongings, you're contributing to a $154 billion industry— bigger than the Hollywood film business!"
—Joshua Becker

Why all this talk about stuff in a chapter on money? Because having too much stuff can actually prevent you from possessing the *right things, the things you need,* in your life. How? Both by not leaving any room for the good stuff and by spending unwisely, which quite literally drains your financial resources. If you are suffering from a stuffed but under-abundant life, if you're drowning in clutter but still feel like there is never enough, it is time to create some space. In the end you let go in order to receive. It's true for love. It's true for money. You have to let go of your fear of the unknown. Let go of your fear that nothing better will come along. Let go of the idea that the only way to show love is to hold on. Let go of the habits that hold you back. Focus on prosperity and look for abundance. It will require a mental shift, and your brain will resist at first, but it's so worth it!

What is prosperity other than a feeling of gratitude for all that you *have* rather than despair over all that you *don't* have? Throughout history, all the great teachers have made gratitude a key principle in their teachings. If you find yourself coming home each evening and cursing your day, your boss, your home, and your life, then that pessimistic, angry, defeated feeling will manifest more of the same and drag you down into more unhappiness. As they say, "A negative mind will never give you a positive life."

Before you lift a finger to make changes in your home, try to flip your thought process. Start with this: Every day as you put your key in the lock of your front door, say "thank you" to your home. If you have to, tape a note to your door as a reminder to say it as you come in. At first you may not mean it, but say it anyway. Tell your front door, your entry table, your kitchen sink, your living room sofa, "Thank you, and I am grateful that you are here to support me." Acknowledge how lucky you are to have each room and each object. Start with rooms and items that are easy to love, or that you at least feel neutral about. If the front entry is driving you to distraction, find something small about it that you *do* like. Maybe the fact that your key turns easily in the lock is enough to be grateful for. I spent a year of my life feeling angry at a sticky lock, so trust me, a well-working lock is a thing to enjoy!

If you're struggling with under-abundance, it may feel bizarre to show appreciation for a life that causes you so much frustration. I am not asking you to sugarcoat your reality, nor am I trying to dismiss hardship you may be experiencing. But as my mother always points out, not only does whining about it do no good, it also makes an unpleasant situation even worse. Why not seek out the good, focus on what you *do* have, and work toward something better? As Rhonda Byrne writes in *The Secret*, "You have to find a way that works for you to focus on prosperity despite the bills around you." Try a slight shift in your thinking, paired with little shifts in your environment, and you will create the opportunity for profound change to occur in your life.

MONEY SCENARIO 3: POWERLESSNESS

> **"Money is only a tool. It will take you**
> **wherever you wish, but it will not**
> **replace you as the driver."**
> **—Ayn Rand**

The third scenario is one that I faced in my first marriage. I trusted my then-husband with all the money and all the money choices. Married to a financial planner, an MBA, and a soon-to-be lawyer, I figured, *What could I possibly know about money that he wouldn't know more about?* The guy tutored me in physics in college—deferring to him made sense to me. At first it didn't seem like a big deal; from the outside, we looked like a couple that made decisions together, like we both had an equal vote. But on the inside, my confidence with money choices diminished more and more with time, and with that diminishing confidence went my sense of self-worth and my ability to contribute to my marriage or the world. Yes, it was *that* big of a deal.

By the time my marriage ended I couldn't even imagine a real career path for myself. Despite holding two bachelors degrees I could only imagine myself in some kind of admin role. As far as relationships were concerned, I aspired to date a series of men who would hopefully find me entertaining enough to keep around for a while. Today I've achieved so much that those thoughts feel alien to who I am. But that was how far my own sense of self-worth had plummeted. The strong, self-assured, happy Rebecca my family had once known seemed to have disappeared, and it started with me not speaking up about money and other choices that greatly affected my life. It's not that my ex made bad decisions; he really was pretty savvy about money. The problem came when I stopped trusting my own instincts, and that lack of trust in myself carried over into every life decision.

Are you living a middle-of-the-road, just "fine" life, but really struggling with your comfort around money? Would you rather pull out your own toenails than have a conversation, much less a confrontation, about money? Do you defer to your spouse about spending, to your boss about your salary, and even to your staff about what they should be paid? Would you rather not think about money, spend money, or have to make any decisions around money?

Every time you abdicate responsibility about money, your power shrinks and your voice fades. You stop speaking up for what you need, want, and deserve. The great news is that when it comes to your home, using it to build your courage and decision-making muscles can be fun! Why not start with choosing a warm, rich wall color for your dining room, something that is just a little scary and stretches your comfort zone? Why not sell that table on Craigslist—the one your sister has guilted you into keeping but refuses to take back? Why not take all the kids' toys out of your bedroom and reclaim your grown-up space? If you have spent long enough failing to speak up, even these low-risk actions may feel scary. But as you flex your mini-courage muscles and see that the sky didn't fall, the muscles will grow, you'll move on to bigger challenges, and before you know it you'll be asking for that raise with confidence.

**Every time we abdicate
responsibility about money,
our power shrinks and our voice fades.**

If you are a money avoider, you may also be a mail avoider. If you fear that a bill lurks in your mail pile, you are likely going to avoid dealing with that pile as if a live snake were nestled in it. One of the ways that your home can help retrain how you see your money situation is for you to set up an intake system for dealing with mail and bills. Stacks of mail cause stress simply by being a pile of the unknown. Humans have a tendency to imagine the worst. This means that a pile of unknown stuff (unopened mail in particular) brings unnecessary stress each day. To avoid that stress, clear the unknown out of your home or, better yet, never let it in in the first place. Be as proactive about what you keep out as what and whom you let in.

In *Apartment Therapy*, Maxwell Gillingham-Ryan writes, "Imagine the front hall as a big filter for the outside world. Many companies make a living trying to get our attention and grab our eyeballs. You should value your time at home highly and not give your eyeballs away easily. Therefore, don't open junk mail. Don't keep magazines or catalogues you haven't ordered. With a good filter, many things may approach, but nothing gets into your home unless it is good for you." So the second you get your hands on your mail, toss what is obviously junk (you'll come to recognize it pretty quickly), immediately open the bills, and list them out to pay them. At first it may be scary knowing what you have to pay, but it is actually less scary and *much* less stressful than *not* knowing and imagining the worst.

EMBRACE TRUE ABUNDANCE

"Wealth is the ability to fully experience life."
—Henry David Thoreau

At some point we have to shed the limits that others have placed on us and the limits we have accepted. We have to say to our friends, our parents, "Your limits are not my limits." Or "Your fear and scarcity are not my fear and scarcity." As you look at what is in your home and see the burden of stuff that you carry, you see the reflection of your own fear and shame, and that of your family too. By letting go of some of the *things*, you also let go of some of the fear.

A happy home makes you feel comfortable with your success and proud of your achievements, even your modest ones. A home that beats you down is just as defeating as a parent who tells you you're not good enough. Maybe it will make you desperate enough to create a change, but desperation rarely leads to the most powerful and positive change. Why not be supported by your home, feel good about the abundance in your life, and speak up with confidence about how and when you will invest time, money, and energy into your life?

FIND YOUR FINANCIAL FREEDOM

No matter which scenario you fall into, if you are dissatisfied with your financial situation, your home can help. You may make plenty of money but still come home to a house that reeks of failure. You may work hard to make ends meet but drown in the overabundance of unnecessary stuff. You might be so afraid of money that it keeps you from a plentiful life. Whichever situation you are in, making changes in your home can help repair and restructure your relationship with money. No matter what you've spent in the past, bought or didn't buy, or held onto until now, it isn't too late to reframe your money mindset. Sure, there is money unaccounted for, and there is stuff you bought that you didn't need. There are objects that remind you of poor spending choices. Put that in the past. Get that stuff out of your home, stop beating yourself up about it, and move forward. It's not doing you any good to throw good money, and good energy, after bad.

Before you move on to the next chapter, take some time with the following exercises to more fully explore your relationship with abundance in your home. Doing these exercises will help you find the clarity to see what brings you satisfaction, the courage to face the music and let things go, and the strength to speak up for what you need from your home, your partner, your boss, and yourself.

Activity 7. Money Matters

This exercise will help you become more aware of the relationship you have with the objects in your home as they relate to money and your sense of wealth. Complete each statement:

Success-o-meter

An object in my home that I define as "expensive" is _____

    That object makes me feel _____

    If that object had cost less I <u>would</u> / <u>would not</u> keep it.

An object in my home that I define as "cheap" is _____

    That object makes me feel _____

    If that object had cost more I <u>would</u> / <u>would not</u> have bought it.

My home <u>does</u> / <u>does not</u> reflect the success I have in my career.

If my boss were to visit my home, I would feel _____
If my colleagues were to visit my home, I would feel _____
When my friends visit my home, I feel _____
When my dates visit my home, I feel _____

Stuff-o-meter

I have <u>too much / just enough / too little</u> stuff in my home.

There <u>are / are not</u> rooms or closets in my home that are hard to enter because they are so full of stuff.

If I felt better about the amount of stuff in my home my life would be different because: _____

Power-o-meter

I personally chose _____% of the stuff in my home because I loved it.

The rest of the stuff and colors were chosen by or for _____

The things that were not chosen by or for me make me feel _____

If there were more of "me" in this house I would feel _____

I last made a spending decision in my home _____

   It was for _____

Activity 8. New Discoveries, Old Habits

Let's explore the ways in which you interacted with abundance as a child, the ways in which you spend now or feel you ought to spend or save, and the ways in which you might start to relate to abundance. In each blank space, write three adjectives that best finish the statement. There are no wrong words.

When I was a child:

Money was _____ , _____ and _____
Gifts we got were _____ , _____ and _____
Gifts we gave were _____ , _____ and _____
We bought important things _____ , _____ and _____
We bought fun things _____ , _____ and _____
We were told to spend _____ , _____ and _____
The things in my room were _____ , _____ and _____

At this time in my life:

Money is _____ , _____ and _____

Gifts I get are _____ , _____ and _____

Gifts I give are _____ , _____ and _____

I buy important things _____ , _____ and _____

I buy fun things _____ , _____ and _____

I spend _____ , _____ and _____

The things in my home are _____ , _____ and _____

In the future in which I want to live:

Money will be _____ , _____ and _____

Gifts I get will be _____ , _____ and _____

Gifts I give will be _____ , _____ and _____

I'll buy important things _____ , _____ and _____

I'll buy fun things _____ , _____ and _____

I'll be able to spend _____ , _____ and _____

The things in my home will be _____ , _____ and _____

Activity 9. Taking Action

Now that you've completed Activity 7 and Activity 8, what have you discovered about your relationship with money and the ways your home affects it? What three things would you like to change? What resources do you need to make those changes? By what date could the changes happen? What is the very first small, tangible step you can take to make progress today?

A change: _____

Date this will happen by (both a date I'd like and that is achievable): _____

Resources I need: _____

A step I can take today: _____

A change: _____

Date this will happen by (both a date I'd like and that is achievable): _____

Resources I need: _____

A step I can take today: _____

A change: _____

Date this will happen by (both a date I'd like and that is achievable): _____

Resources I need: _____

A step I can take today: _____

TO SUM UP

To experience abundance (in terms of money, belongings, relationships, and time) connect with the meaning behind your money and possessions. If you work hard but come home to a space that feels void of love and warmth, there may be a disconnect between your professional success and your home life. When you feel simultaneously overwhelmed by stuff and also lacking in abundance, it's like eating a big meal without nutrition. You feel stuffed but not satisfied. And if you let others decide how and where you live and what you spend, you quickly lose sight of your self-worth. Learning to edit what comes into your home, having a say in what surrounds you, and practicing mindfulness around purchases is a surefire way to exercise your abundance and prosperity muscles. Start practicing now, and in time you will surely face big decisions with courage and confidence.

Chapter 3.
Happy and Healthy: Living a Fit and Energetic Lifestyle

*"He who has health, has hope; and he
who has hope, has everything."*
—Thomas Carlyle

EVERY YEAR LOSING WEIGHT and getting fit ranks in the top five New Year's resolutions. If you're one of the many seeking a healthier lifestyle, there are countless ways your home can help you achieve that goal. In fact, modifying your physical environment can be one of the most effective ways to change a habit and break free from self-destructive patterns.

If you've been struggling for years to sleep better, exercise more, stop smoking, or change some other behavior, adjusting your physical environment might be the element that finally tips the scales and makes all your effort pay off. A so-called "geographical cure" puts you in a space that changes the cues you've been getting that support your negative habit. This can work for even the most addictive habits. In fact, the success of the so-called geographical cure was demonstrated in a study of Vietnam veterans. Despite the heroin habit the study subjects had formed during their service overseas, the majority of the servicemen in the study successfully quit their addictions when they returned home. In short, when they changed their environment, they left behind the cues that triggered their drug habit, and this made their rehabilitation much more successful.

If a geographical cure can help people recover from addictions, why not use it on other habits that drag us down in life? If changing the environment is a way to break free from a drug addiction, think of how it can help you give up a cookie habit, or help you build a new pattern of daily walks. What if a simple thing like changing your kitchen paint color could wake up your subconscious and override any thoughtless habits you have formed?

The important thing to understand is this: if you are ready to transform your habits and change your life, *not* redesigning your space can actually *sabotage* your best efforts. In your old space you are constantly cued to keep your old habits. In your "new" environment you're no longer surrounded by all those reminders. You are free to create a new reality for yourself!

SHORT-CIRCUIT OLD PATTERNS AND BUILD NEW HABITS

It should come as no surprise that it is hard to stop smoking or drinking when you keep finding yourself in the same situation in which you used to drink or smoke. Like Pavlov's dog, you see, hear, and smell the cues and then salivate for the reward. You must change what you sense around you in order to short-circuit the system and rewire your brain for a new way of behaving. Does that mean you have to physically leave your home and move to a new neighborhood? Not necessarily. You can create a space that will send new signals to your brain—and, therefore, transform your daily patterns—just by making changes to your present environment.

When you are building new habits, every tiny obstacle is like having Mount Everest between where you are and where you want to be. Remove as many obstacles as you can, and you will exponentially increase your chances of success. When you eliminate the things that trigger old habits, it's easier to make healthy choices.

For better health, including reducing weight and stress, try making these three changes in your home: First, make the tools you need (workout clothes, running shoes, bike, etc.) accessible so you can get outside without too much effort. Second, clear out the kitchen so that it is easier to choose and prepare healthy food, and create a dining space where you can focus on food and family, not on TV. Third, cross items off your household to-do list to elim-inate unconscious stress, since stress leads to physical pain, comfort eating, and sleep disturbances.

ONE: GET A MOVE ON

**"An early-morning walk is a blessing for
the whole day." —Henry David Thoreau**

We all know we *should* get outside more. Nonetheless, most of us are in the habit of hitting the snooze alarm in the morning, and then at the end of the day trudging to the fridge instead of jogging to the park. It's even worse on dark, cold, wet winter mornings, or when it takes more work to find your running shoes than it's worth. If better health is a priority for you, here are some changes you can make.

First, transform the visual and physical cues in your home. Say you have a habit of going to the pantry right after work and eating a handful of cookies. If you've indulged this habit for a while, chances are it has become somewhat unconscious. That means you have to shake things up to trigger some awareness around the habit. For three weeks, keep the cookies somewhere else in the house (like in the garage) and put your iPod in the pantry where you normally keep the cookies. Each time you go to the pantry you'll see the iPod, which you can grab and take on a quick walk before you eat the cookies. Yes, you can still eat the cookies, but take the walk first. After the walk, if you still want cookies, go ahead. Of course you'll have to detour to the garage to get them, and that is important: this makes your choice *conscious* instead of unconscious. Do this for at least twenty-one days. It takes that long to build a new habit (or break an old one).

**By their very nature habits are
unconscious. If making healthier choices
is a priority, make changes in your home
to make your patterns concious again.**

If you work from home and your tendency is to flip on the TV during your lunch break, move the remote to your sock drawer (again, just for three weeks) so you're forced to turn the TV on manually. Next to the TV power button, post a sticky note that reminds you to ride your stationary bike for twenty minutes.

You might end up turning the TV on four out of five days, but if just one day a week you change that habit, you are well on your way to a new lifestyle.

If you hit the snooze button three times every morning for those extra thirty minutes of sleep, consider putting your alarm or phone across the room so you have to get up to hit snooze. Have your gym clothes already folded under the phone. Once you stumble out of bed, you'll increase your chances of stumbling into those gym clothes and getting out for a walk.

When I needed to break my hot-cocoa-in-the-evenings habit, I moved the cocoa mix to the lowest corner of the pantry, way back behind the flour. Having to work just a little bit harder to reach it helped me create a conscious choice around something that had turned into a comforting ritual. It worked better than I expected, and I didn't drink hot cocoa for a whole week (that is, until my husband forgot to put the mix back in the hiding spot and I made myself a cup). Out of sight, out of mind.

Any visual or physical cue that jogs your attention and compels you to make a decision, rather than act on habit, will work. For example, one of my clients wanted to reduce her TV-watching time, so we swapped the position of the sofa and loveseat in her living room—sitting in a new location woke her up to a new choice. Another client placed a giant stuffed bunny in the pantry, which made her chuckle, and the laughter itself did more to relieve some of her stress than a handful of Oreos. Another client wanted to stop checking her email and social media accounts right before bed (a habit which has been proven to disrupt sleep quality), so I suggested she move the charger to a different room.

In addition to creating new visual cues in your home, make sure your tools are readily accessible. If you have home gym equipment, remember that it is only any good if you *use it*. So be brutally honest with yourself about what you will, or won't, use. If you stick the treadmill in the darkest, dankest corner of your basement, will you really go down there? If you aren't using your equipment, sell what you've got and find something that will work. Never waste precious home real estate on useless equipment. It will just make you feel bad and sabotage your health efforts. Who needs the stress? Even if five years ago you used that elliptical machine religiously, it's okay to let it go if it's no longer your thing—we all get tired of doing the same thing year after year. Consider selling it and buying another machine. Worried about how much you spent on it? Well, if you are not using the machine you're wasting the money anyway, so you might as well accept it and move on.

It's not just the big tools (like bikes, strollers, home workout equipment) that you need to have readily accessible. The small tools (running shoes, workout clothes, yoga mat, and the like) are just as important. Can you find your running shoes, or are they buried in the coat closet under a dozen pairs of kids' shoes, mismatched mittens, and coats that no longer fit anyone in the household? When you wake up to rain, do you have a ready-to-grab hat and jacket nearby? Clear out that coat closet and put back *only* the things that are essential for your healthy-living habits. Where will you put all that other junk that accumulated there—the Nerf guns, rollerblades, and souvenir umbrellas? It doesn't matter. Stick them in the garage for now, focus on the goal at hand, and don't let a question like that get in the way of building new habits for the next three weeks. One bite of the elephant at a time, as they say.

Finally, clear out your workout clothes drawer. Three tops, three bottoms, three bras, five pairs of socks—that is plenty. They should *all* fit, and they should *all* make you feel good. Ditch the 1980s spandex and the 1970s mini shorts. Sure, they still "work," but you're unlikely to wear them and they are just getting in the way. Your exercise clothing drawer should be so organized that you could get dressed in the dark and feel confident that you'll be leaving the house in a top, bottom, and socks that are in good repair, fit well, and look like they are from this decade. Remember, every little obstacle is Mount Everest when you are building new patterns. Conquer every hurdle you can *before* the 6 a.m. alarm goes off.

It goes without saying that physical exercise and time spent outdoors improves our well-being, and that failing to make time for it can lead to bad posture, weight gain, and increased chances of depression. Your home can either make it easy to get outside and get a move on, or it can make it hard. Change up what you see, get your tools in order, and get ready to build new habits. Just clearing out your coat closet so it doesn't take twenty minutes to find a set of mittens on a wintry day will increase your chances of success.

TWO: COOK UP SOME NEW EATING HABITS

> "One cannot think well, love well, sleep
> well, if one has not dined well."
> —Virginia Woolf

It's great to move your body, except when it comes time to eat. When you eat, you should slow down, relax, and enjoy. Let's talk about ways to make cooking at home easier so you have time to sit down and savor what you've prepared. And if healthy eating is your goal, then just like with your easy-to-grab walking clothes, you need a kitchen that is easy to use. Clear out the kitchen so you can easily choose and prepare healthy food, and create spaces to eat where you can focus on food and family, not on the TV.

We all know the healthiest way to eat is to prepare meals at home from fresh ingredients. Before you protest that you just don't have the time, know that studies have shown that prepackaged foods don't save more than about five minutes of cooking time when preparing a midweek dinner. You actually save time by planning meals ahead. And if you can commit to meal strategizing for three weeks, the planning will come quickly as you find a set of recipes that are comfortable, quick, and easy to buy and prepare. If you are brand new to meal planning, consider hiring a health coach during your three-week habit-changing period. Remember: the time you think you are saving now by purchasing prepackaged food may cost you later in doctors' bills and hospital visits.

For now, let's just be sure your home makes it easy to do the work. Start by clearing the clutter from the cabinets and the counters. Get rid of what you don't need. If your counters don't have any workspace, and if your basic pans, knives, and cutting boards aren't easy to reach, you'll have to climb Mount Impossible before you've even retrieved your first ingredient.

If you are serious about eating more nutritiously, create cooking and eating spaces that support your goals.

Begin with the obvious—the stuff that doesn't belong in your kitchen in the first place: the junk mail, the art projects, the box of stuff meant for charity. Then get brutal about the kitchen "toys": the juicers, dehydrators, speedy ovens, mandolin slicers, countertop roasters, microwave bacon bowls, and other As Seen On TV gizmos. These supposedly magical gadgets are all fighting for space on your counter. In all likelihood not a single one is getting used, and meanwhile you have no space left to actually cook. For now, box it all up, put it in the garage, and put a date on the calendar two months from now. If, by that date, you have not gone to the garage to retrieve *and use* an item, take the whole box to Goodwill. Meanwhile, stick to the basics: Learn to use a decent chef's knife, a paring knife, a skillet, and a soup pan. Add to that a colander and a chopping board, and that is enough to cook almost any healthy meal you can conceive. If you can afford it, invest in quality versions of these essentials, especially a nice, sharp eight- or ten-inch chef's knife. Durable, functional tools make it much easier to become a comfortable cook.

Once you have the kitchen in working order (probably by clearing out 50 percent of the stuff—do you really need sixty mismatched plastic food containers, half of which are missing lids?), create a peaceful, TV-free space in your home where you can eat meals. It may sound obvious, but start with a comfortable table and chairs. According to nutritionist and health coach Aimee Gallo of Vibrance Nutrition and Fitness, sitting allows your body to focus on the job of digestion and encourages you to slow down so that you taste and enjoy the food. By banning the distractions (TV, books, computer) you'll be aware of what you are eating and pay attention to your body as it tells you when it is full. You end up eating less and enjoying more. Eating foods that you find delicious goes hand in hand with cooking fresh food and banishing cardboard-style diet foods from your life. If you are serious about eating more nutritiously, create cooking and eating spaces that support your goals.

A REMODELING REMEDY

Sometimes these small changes—clearing the clutter, reducing kitchen equipment to only the essentials—are all that's required to make healthy cooking easier. Sometimes a more dramatic change may be in order. Don't discount the power of a remodel. One of my recently retired clients, Mary, had been told by her doctor that if she didn't make dramatic changes to her health, she'd be dead within a couple of years. Mary realized that restaurant meals had to stop and that she and her husband would be spending a lot more time cooking and eating at home, so she hired me to help make over her kitchen, dining, and living spaces.

On her own, Mary changed her diet and worked diligently to lose weight. Meanwhile, we worked together to create a space that felt like the home she'd always wanted and a kitchen that made it fun and easy to prepare healthy meals. She lost the weight her doctor recommended and a year later had kept it all off. In end she said, "You made all this possible. You helped create a home that feels so wonderful that we don't even want to eat out. We love being here. Even my husband looks around and says what a nice place we have. Because we love it here, it's easy to avoid all those restaurant meals. This home makes it possible to be healthy."

An easy-to-use kitchen will make your healthy-eating goals possible. That doesn't always mean you need a remodel, but if you *do* remodel, it is important to map out your long-term goals as part of the project. At the start of most projects, my clients' kitchens are usually stuffed with food that is unhealthy and kitchen gadgets that sold a dream but failed to deliver. If they'd just moved all that stuff back into their new, beautiful kitchens, they'd have spent a lot of money but not done the work they need to truly reinvent their lives. So even if you do plan to remodel your kitchen, you *still* have to do the work of clearing out the tools and food that sabotage your long-term goals.

DESTROY THE DAILY STRESSORS

> **"When you have a great and difficult task, something perhaps almost impossible, if you only work a little at a time, every day a little, suddenly the work will finish itself." —Isak Dinesen**

The last change to make in your home is to reduce stressors, which can come at you in the form of a mile-long to-do list, the threat of uncertainty, or a health crisis, among many others.

Let's start with something you can pretty easily take control of: working your way through that household to-do list. Fix the broken doorknob, repaint the shabby front door, repair the dripping faucet. Stress alone can make you sick (according to the American Psychological Association, 73 percent of people in the United States regularly experience physical symptoms caused by stress), and incomplete tasks can create an unconscious stress. Unconscious stress not only makes it feel like you never have permission to rest, but also takes a toll on your energy and coping skills so that when you need to address a big stressor in your life, you deplete the reserves left to handle it well. Stress causes physical pain, leads to comfort eating, and disturbs sleep. So you benefit by getting rid of every little stress that you can. Complete just one home repair a week, and within a month you'll find yourself feeling calmer and more in control of your emotions and home life.

For most of us, that home to-do list also includes decluttering or getting organized, and this is a very important part of feeling less stressed at home. Just like people, houses often gain weight over time. As Maxwell Gillingham-Ryan writes in *Apartment Therapy*, "When we take something new into our home, we rarely let go of something else. This is how our home gains weight, grows unhealthy, and begins to nag at us . . . Most of us aren't in need of more organizing; we need to manage our consumption, let go of our stuff, and learn how to restore life to our homes."

Clutter, even when stuffed out of sight in closets and garages, takes up space in our brains and adds bulk to our lives, pulling us down, making us feel less capable and more stressed, and leading us to habits of overeating, under-sleeping, and couch-potato-ing. When I work with clients to create a healthier home, I remind them that I am not an "organizer"; I am a "releaser." I (kindly but firmly) help clients let go of stuff that weighs them down and keeps the good stuff from getting in.

Clutter, even when stuffed out of sight in closets and garages, takes up space in our brains and makes us feel stressed.

You know that if you fill up on junk food, there is no room left for whole foods. In the same way, if you fill your home with stuff that people hand you but you don't want and with junk that you bought on sale, there is no room left in your home for quality possessions that bring you love and joy. You end up surrounded by stuff but void of anything of value. Your eating, exercising, and general health habits follow suit.

If you have a history of junk-food-style living, if your home is more hand-me-downs than intentional design, don't let that worry you. As James Ray said in *The Secret*, "Most people look at their current state of affairs and they say, 'This is who I am.' That's not who you are. That's who you *were*." Your past is important, because it brought you to where you are today and made you strong and resilient, but it has no bearing on how you will live from this moment forward.

So ask yourself, "How would *future me* live?" Imagine yourself healthy. Really take a moment to see yourself as that person, living that healthy lifestyle. What do you eat? With whom do you spend your time? What do you read? When do you go to bed, and when do you get up? Once you have a clear picture of *future you*, take a look at your home. That is the home of *past you*. Would *future you* live in this house? If not, it's time for some changes. Adjust the environment of *past you* to fit the environment of *future you*, and see how simple it is to actually slip into that new way of being.

A SAFE HOME IS A HAPPY HOME

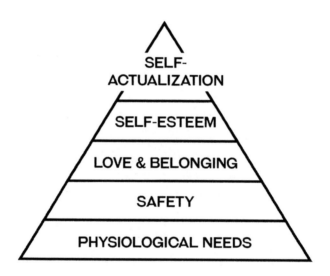

The final element to discuss in this chapter on being healthy is our need for security and safety. In Maslow's hierarchy of needs, safety and security is second in line only to our basic physiological needs of food, shelter, and breathing. The stress of feeling unsafe, insecure, or out of control can take a serious toll on your health and on your family's health. This can be especially important after big changes like divorce, a major illness, or the death of a family member. A sense of safety can also be disrupted by a home invasion or a robbery. Literal physical safety in your home contributes to your health and well-being. It's important to make sure you have a home that contributes to a sense of security and safety, stability, and permanence.

A HEALTHY HOME IS A HAPPY HOME

Your home environment (and for that matter, your workplace) is the essential foundation to your health and well-being. The great news is that no matter where you live you can shape the space in a way that benefits you and helps you change destructive habits. The impact of our spaces simply can't be dismissed. It has been well studied in hospital environments that the physical space even impacts our ability to heal after our health has been compromised. In *A Whole New Mind*, Daniel Pink says this:

> Most hospitals and doctors' offices are not exactly repositories of charm and good taste. And while physicians and administrators might favor changing that state of affairs, they generally consider it secondary to the more pressing matters of prescribing drugs and performing surgery. But a growing body of evidence is showing that improving the design of medical settings helps patients get better faster. For example, in a study at Pittsburgh's Montefiore Hospital, surgery patients in rooms with ample natural light required less pain medication, and their drug costs were 21 percent lower, than their counterparts in traditional rooms. Another study compared two groups of patients who suffered identical ailments. One group was treated in a drab conventional ward of the hospital. The other was treated in a modern, sunlit, visually appealing ward. Patients in the better-designed ward needed less pain medicine than those in the less inviting ward and were discharged on average nearly two days early.

Nothing reminds us of the importance of our well-being more than a serious health crisis. Unfortunately none of us are immune to illness, but we can create homes that help us maintain good health and recover more quickly when we do face sickness. Study after study shows that patients in hospitals with windows to the outside world, rooms and lighting that allow for natural sleep patterns, and spaces that allow for soft engagement between people help patients heal more quickly and use less pain medication. Why not support your health with a home that helps you make nourishing choices and heal more quickly if you do fall ill?

I worked with a busy client, Brenda, about a year after she'd moved into her home. She and her husband called me to help furnish their empty house so they could start entertaining again. As we were getting started, Brenda ended up needing heart surgery. So, unfortunately, it turned out we needed to first focus on creating a home for healing instead of for entertaining. After we finished furnishing and decorating, Brenda followed up with this note: "At least I have a beautifully decorated home to look at while I sit on my ever-so-comfy sofa! . . . [We] really have made a house a home, a comfortable resting area, and a joy to live in."

None of us are guaranteed perfect health at all times, but we can certainly create spaces where we can heal, and live, in peace.

Activity 10. On Guard: Creating a Sense of Safety and Permanence

Take a quick assessment of your home using the following checklist:

Safety:
- ☐ My windows and doors have secure and easy-to-use locks.
- ☐ My windows have easy-to-operate shades or curtains to maintain privacy at night.
- ☐ My windows and doors are easy to open in case of a fire or an intruder.
- ☐ I can see who is at my door without opening it.
- ☐ I know the names of my neighbors and how to reach them in an emergency.
- ☐ I have checked the fire alarms in my home and have fire extinguishers near heat sources.
- ☐ I know where to find the shutoff for the water and gas.
- ☐ My family has an out-of-the-home, agreed-upon gathering spot in case of emergency.

Permanence:
- ☐ I know when the people in my house plan to leave and return home.
- ☐ There are no unpacked boxes in my home suggesting we might move at any time.
- ☐ There is art and other décor hung on the walls, indicating we plan to stay here.

Once you complete Activity 10, note the elements that you were not able to check off and create a plan on the calendar for how you will address each one. Before moving on to the next activity or chapter, accomplish at least one task. I promise you'll feel better when you take action!

Activity 11. Health Hunt

How ready is your home for the new, healthy you? Set a timer for fifteen minutes, and get ready to hunt down all the essentials you need to create healthy habits. (This one is fun to do with the kids too!)

- ☐ Skillet
- ☐ Soup pan
- ☐ Spatula
- ☐ Eight- or ten-inch chef's knife (bonus if it's sharp!)
- ☐ Paring knife
- ☐ Cutting board for veggies
- ☐ Cutting board for meats
- ☐ Colander
- ☐ Measuring spoons
- ☐ Measuring cups
- ☐ At least two feet of clear counter space
- ☐ Comfy walking or running shoes
- ☐ Comfortable walking pants or shorts
- ☐ Comfortable walking shirt
- ☐ Lightweight rain jacket
- ☐ Rain and sun hat
- ☐ Gloves
- ☐ Sunscreen
- ☐ Water bottle
- ☐ Music source (cell phone/iPod/MP3 player) with charged batteries and headphones
- ☐ A clutter-free bedroom with light and sound control
- ☐ A comfortable bed that supports your back and your sleep

When the fifteen minutes are up, look at the objects you were able to find. Got them all? Great! No excuses: start your meal planning and exercise regimen right away. Got about half? No worries: take an extra fifteen minutes to finish gathering what you missed, and start your meal planning and exercise regimen immediately. Missing most of them? That's okay too. Instead of starting your regimen tomorrow, create a shopping list and a plan for getting what you need, and consider enlisting a little help, since you are starting from scratch. No need to buy top-of-the-line for everything; just make it good enough to support, and not sabotage, your goals. If you're on a tight budget, start with secondhand stuff. The investment really will pay off! You are, quite literally, putting your money where your mouth is.

Activity 12. Taking Action

Now that you've read this chapter, what three things would you like to change to be healthier? What resources do you need to make those changes happen? By what date could the changes happen? What is the very first small, tangible step you can take to make progress today?

A change: _____

Date this will happen by (both a date I'd like and that is achievable): _____
Resources I need: _____
A step I can take today: _____

A change: _____

Date this will happen by (both a date I'd like and that is achievable): _____
Resources I need: _____
A step I can take today: _____

A change: _____

Date this will happen by (both a date I'd like and that is achievable): _____
Resources I need: _____
A step I can take today: _____

TO SUM UP

Our spaces affect our health. We can design them to help us heal faster. We can adjust them to help us change our habits. We can update them to make it easier to make healthy choices. The only thing we can't do is ignore the impact our spaces have on our well-being. We can choose to take action, but avoiding change means leaving a powerful tool on the table.

Chapter 4.
Happy and Well-Rested:
Renewing through Sound Sleep

"Sleep is the best meditation."
—the Dalai Lama

AS I WRITE THIS BOOK AND START EACH CHAPTER, I keep thinking, "Oh! This is the Most Important Thing." Creative play, personal growth, good health . . . all topics worthy of our attention. In the end, however, without sleep, rest, and renewal, none of the other pursuits are even possible. Without restorative sleep and rest, life becomes unbearable. Everything feels hard. Life just sucks.

On the other hand, when we are rested, we are able to focus and accomplish more. We are energetic, positive, and powerful. We are more generous, kind, and tolerant. We have more patience, less brain fog, and a sense of well-being. One simply cannot overstate the power of restful sleep. And not just sleep. Rest doesn't just happen at bedtime. There also has to be downtime during the day. In our Go! Go! Go! world we often forget to simply breathe, to just be. All that constant running around wears down our ability to cope, to handle the Big Things when they come along.

TOO MUCH INPUT

Most of us are *overstimulated* and, at any age, overstimulation creates irritable, intolerant people. We are not built to be constantly bombarded with noise, light, and information, and in fact it can have a severely damaging effect. As adults, we think we are equipped to absorb the daily damage of stress and overstimulation, and we trick ourselves into thinking we're "fine." But the truth is revealed when we look at more vulnerable creatures.

In the 1960s, research started showing that sensory deprivation in young animals led to developmental problems later. With that emerging science, caretakers of premature babies started wondering if preemies in neonatal intensive care centers needed more attention. The thought was that perhaps more stimulation would help them develop and grow stronger more quickly. In her research for *The Power of Place*, Winifred Gallagher discovered that, in fact, premature babies don't need more stimulation, but rather they often get *too much* input. With lights on at all times and music playing all night to keep nurses awake and alert, "trying to develop in an NICU is like trying to live in a busy airport or subway station. The problem isn't that these places offer too little [stimulation], but, in a particularly modern way, too much." As a result, as described by developmental psychologist William Fifer, "[the preemies] are much more irritable. Their cries are very shrill . . . Later on, they're likelier to have more developmental and learning problems." We all need shelter from this chaotic and busy world. That happens through quiet, sleep, and rest. And just because we adults have more coping mechanisms than preemies doesn't make it any less true for us.

It's not just audible noise that wears us down, but also the "noise" from too much clutter and too many projects, all demanding: *Pay attention to me!*

From day one, we all need time to sleep, rest, and recover from the input around us. As I said, while adults may be better equipped than infants to cope with noise, even grown-ups are profoundly affected by constant stimuli. It's not just audible noise that wears us down (blaring radios, TVs, video games, cell phones, traffic outside, voices inside), but also the "noise" from too much clutter, too many colors, too many piles to sort, too many half-finished projects—all screaming, *Pay attention to me!* It is no wonder we retreat into the world of our televisions, numbing our brains and bodies with junk TV and junk food.

Of course, it's possible to be under-stimulated too, but in all honesty, this is a rare problem for most Americans. But regardless of whether we are facing over- or under-stimulation, just as in the study of premature babies, the question really is this: What is the best kind and amount of stimulation *for you*?

REDUCING THE NUMBER OF VOICES SHOUTING AT US

If you're like most American adults—overscheduled and overstimulated—you need an environment that helps you worry less and sleep more. Where to start?

Sometimes it means checking off your to-do list and eliminating some of the tasks around your home that need attention. A door that is a bit hard to open or a lock that is difficult to turn means extra effort in your day, and that suggests that life is a struggle. Yet a sticky door is the kind of little annoyance that we never quite get to, and a dozen of those "little things" grate on us and make it just that much harder to handle the big stuff. When a dozen little things require just a little more effort, it adds up to an overall depletion in the energy that you need to manage your day, and ultimately to deal with the Big Things. On the other hand, if you take one task off the list each week, within a few weeks you might find yourself facing less of an uphill battle each day, more able to deal gracefully with life's challenges.

We often create our own frustrating realities.

I spent a year getting angry every single time I came home because my front door lock didn't work well. Every afternoon I'd start out hoping that my husband had made it home before me and had left the door unlocked. He would often get home ahead of me, but out of a sense of security he would lock the door behind him. (Yes, that was reasonable, but it didn't *feel* reasonable at the time.) Then I'd get angry at him for not leaving it unlocked for me (*He should have just sensed that I was almost home!*). In frustration I would set down my belongings and use one hand to pull the door toward me and the other hand to turn the key. By the time I'd unlocked that stupid door, gathered my bags, and walked inside, my blood was at a boil. Every night I'd scream in my head: *Why can't he just leave the door unlocked? Why can't he be bothered to change the lock set? Why is everything SO HARD?*

It was ridiculous. I had a lovely home, an amazing husband, and a great life. Luckily, one day I woke up to the fact that *I was creating this frustrating reality.* I had the power to change the situation. On my way home that night, I popped into my local home improvement store, got a new lockset, gathered all the tools, and changed out the lock. Twenty minutes, done. Ever since, coming home has been a breeze. Why couldn't I see that solution earlier?

Since that small success I have made it a habit to regularly address the small home maintenance needs around my house—burnt-out lightbulbs, dirty walls, dishwasher drips. Trust me, if you tend to them while they are still minor, no-big-deal issues, they won't become a big deal. Why live with broken windows, dusty blinds, and frayed welcome mats? Small fixes, big relief!

LEARNING TO RELAX

For most of my life I've heard this advice over and over again: "You should just relax," and "Don't worry so much." Well, relaxing just doesn't come naturally to me. I fit right into our culture of *Go! Go! Go!* and *Do! Do! Do!* It turns out that I am not alone: many of us find it hard to relax. Even when we try to relax, we often get it wrong. Mihaly Csikszentmihalyi, author of *Flow: The Psychology of Optimal Experience*, found that "when we try to relax, instead of ending up at an optimum level of stimulation, we overshoot. We wind up in a state of apathy, which is what most people report when watching TV. After a stressful day at work, they pass a dull night in front of the television."

We all need to find a way to balance the highs and lows of our lives and create a place of centered being. Maybe for you that means a change in habit, or maybe something bigger like a change in career. Maybe it means you need more support from your family and a little time away. To make the *right* change, first sort through what is not working, what is driving you crazy, and what an optimum environment and day would feel like to you. A well-balanced life is like a sleek, high-end car: It's pleasing, simple to use, easy to maintain, and supportive of the body. As with the car, so with your home. As with your home, so with your life. When we lack information about when and where we feel our best, when we put up with drab offices with energy-draining fluorescent lighting and dysfunctional kitchens that make cooking a chore, we invite unnecessary chaos into our lives and feel worn out before we've even tackled the hard stuff. It doesn't have to be that way.

THE VALUE OF A GOOD NIGHT'S SLEEP

"Let her sleep, for when she wakes
she will move mountains."
—Napoleon Bonaparte

In addition to creating a home that eases the burden of the day, you also need regular, restful, complete nights of sleep. Insomnia is a miserable condition, and while sometimes you may need the intervention of Western medicine to reset the chemistry of your body, the design of your bedroom can impact your ability to sleep well.

There are three main areas over which we have direct influence in our bedrooms: the amount of light and noise, our emotional associations, and meta-messages. Let's address those now.

THE POWER OF THE DARK SIDE

Our bodies are designed to respond to light and darkness as cues for being awake and asleep, but the modern age makes it easy to mess with that natural clock. Luckily, the same interior lighting that has overridden our natural sleep habits can also be a tool for resetting our sleep schedule. Instead of turning to a sleeping pill, you can use light to create a natural sleep response in your body. Even if you face a busy city street with bright lights, rumbling traffic, and blaring sirens, you can hang felt-lined blackout curtains, which have an amazing sound-softening and light-deadening effect. Blackout curtains don't have to be expensive or custom-made: a sturdy rod and a pair of off-the-shelf curtains can be plenty.

Try blocking out the streetlights for bedtime, and then consider putting a soft light (something very low, about the brightness of a single candle) on a timer so that it comes on a few minutes before your alarm goes off. That subtle brightening of light will serve as a natural alarm, and you may even find yourself feeling awake by the time the alarm sounds. As soon as you wake up, open the curtains to let in the daylight, and you'll be using your body's natural rhythms to foster good sleep. (If short winter days or a nighttime work schedule mean that there is no daylight when you wake up, turn on several bright lamps after you get out of bed to simulate that daylight effect.)

Besides physically controlling light and noise, use the geography of your home to influence your sleep patterns. In *The Power of Place*, the author summarizes research conducted by psychiatrist Daniel Kripke, a light expert at the University of California at San Diego, who says, "It's amazing how . . . rooms that seem virtually identical can differ greatly in terms of light. For example, people who sleep in bedrooms that have windows that face East are apt to get up earlier and sleep less than those in bedrooms with Western exposure." That means, then, that you can take some control of your sleep patterns not only through window treatments but also through the position of your bedroom in your home. Maybe your bedroom faces west, but you struggle to get up in the mornings, even on the brightest summer days. Try sleeping in an east-facing room for a couple of weeks and see if that makes a difference. Or, if your schedule requires late nights and you need to sleep later, try the western side of the house and make good use of blackout drapes.

We all know that pulling the blinds and dimming the lights helps kids nap in the middle of the day, and opening the blinds and turning up the lights helps them wake up again. Controlling the lighting in your home can have a dramatic impact on your ability to sleep and to wake refreshed. It's as true for you as it is for the kids.

ANXIETY IN THE BEDROOM

> "I've always envied people who sleep
> easily. Their brains must be cleaner,
> the floorboards of the skull well swept,
> all the little monsters closed up in a
> steamer trunk at the foot of the bed."
> —David Benioff, *City of Thieves*

While light and sound control can help us sleep better, the emotional associations you have with your bedroom can dramatically impede your ability to get a good night of sleep. One of my clients went through a divorce and found it distressing to go to bed in the same room that she had once shared with her ex. As part of her healing, she chose to turn the master bedroom into her home office and the guest room into her bedroom. After she made the swap, she had a much easier time falling into a peaceful sleep.

When I went through my divorce, I decided to sell my queen-size bed and buy a twin instead. I wanted to send a message to the universe, loud and clear, that this was a bed for *one*. I also painted the room a pale pink, reinforcing a no-boys-allowed message. I needed a cocoon for a while before I was going to let anyone into my space again.

Even if you are in an established, solid relationship, it's possible that you associate anxiety with your bedroom. Many couples find that the only time they really get together are those last moments of the day as they crawl into bed, and so that is when they end up having intense conversations about money, debt, the kids, his mother, her sister, and whether he should quit his job. If those conversations are fraught and argumentative, a couple will associate anger, frustration, blame, and other anxiety-inducing emotions with the bedroom. If this is happening in your home, try to carve out some time together earlier in the evening. Maybe pause for a cup of tea together in the kitchen after the kids have gone to bed, just to clear the news of the day, and agree to stop the conversation before you head to bed. Take "never go to bed angry" a step further, and try never to enter the bedroom angry, either.

VOICES IN THE BEDROOM

Besides light and noise and negative associations, the meta-messages in your room can also potentially disturb sleep. A meta-message is the underlying information you receive from a room. On the surface, it's a bedroom. But the room's implicit message might be that you are sleeping in a workroom, storage room, or toy room— which, in turn, comes with the expectation that you *should* be addressing the work, the to-do list, or the kids. So what is your bedroom saying to you? If it is filled with paperwork, old magazines, junk mail, kids' toys, piles of laundry, unpacked boxes, and the bed you once shared with your ex, your bedroom is probably sending you these messages:

1. You have no time for sleep and should feel guilty for not getting some of this stuff done.
2. You don't deserve rest and are not worthy of a place for rest.
3. You are stuck in your past and won't ever be able to move on to new and wonderful things.

Wow! And you expect to get a good night's sleep listening to all that garbage? If this is you, it's time for a clean sweep. Banish everything that is unrelated to sleep or sex. Be brutal. Remember, without sleep, none of the other Good Stuff in life is even possible. But *with* a good night of sleep you can conquer the world!

WAKING UP REFRESHED

Clearly it's important to go to bed in an environment that encourages and promotes good sleep. It is just as important to wake up to a positive and happy space. If the first thing you see each day makes you smile and eases you into the day, it's much easier to start out on the right foot.

In *The Secret*, Rhonda Byrne describes her morning ritual of gratitude. From the moment she wakes up, with every step she takes from her bed to the bathroom, she says "thank you" to the universe. She starts her day filled, and filling, with joy and appreciation. If you are trying to develop a similar habit of gratitude, joy, and meditation, why make it any harder on yourself by having a room filled with obstacles? Get the kids' toys out of the bedroom. Put a large enough nightstand by your bed so it's easy to set down your water glass without a precarious balancing act. Fix the closet door so you don't have to struggle with it first thing in the morning. Repair the sink faucet so the water doesn't drip. You may not be able to control what will happen that day, but if you keep your bedroom and bathroom in good repair, and create a soft, sensual, even flattering environment, you won't be wasting your energy first thing in the day, and you'll find yourself more well-equipped to handle the challenges life will throw your way.

Activity 13. Sleep Study

Make a list of the rooms in your home in two groups. In the first group, list the rooms that you think "should" be restful. Perhaps your bedroom, master bathroom, and living room. In the second group list the rooms you wouldn't normally associate with being restful; label these the "energetic" rooms. Perhaps the kids' bathroom, the kitchen, the garage, and the family room.

Next, note whether the room is *actually* restful to you. Don't take for granted that a room that "should" be restful actually *is* restful. For example, one of my clients regularly wakes up in the middle of the night and moves to the sofa or guest room because her husband snores so loudly. Another client slept in a room that was so filled with clutter that only one of them could fit on the king-size bed. The other slept on the sofa. Neither client could have called their bedrooms "restful."

"Restful" Rooms in my Home	Restful?
_____	Yes / No
_____	Yes / No
_____	Yes / No
_____	Yes / No
_____	Yes / No

"Energetic" Rooms in my Home	Restful?
_____	Yes / No
_____	Yes / No
_____	Yes / No
_____	Yes / No
_____	Yes / No

Review the list. Any surprises? If you do not have at least one room in the house that you can clearly and definitively call "restful," it might be time to make some changes. Your home absolutely must give you a place to recharge, or it's not doing its job.

Activity 14. Sleep Vacation

It's time to take a field trip. If you can afford it, book a night at a lovely hotel. You don't have to go far, a staycation in your own city is perfect. From the moment you slide your room key in the lock, take an inventory of your surroundings. How are the furnishings arranged? What creates a feeling of calm? What feels jarring or out of place? Take some time to journal on the things that make this space different from your home space, including features that you might actually want to adapt in your own bedroom.

If an overnight hotel stay isn't in your budget, look at pictures of hotel rooms online instead. Note which rooms appeal to you. Are they elegant? Lodge-like? Beachy? Colorful? Neutral? One of my favorite overnight stays was at the Opus in Vancouver, BC. The walls were painted a deep ocean blue that made me feel calm and grounded, and the modern furniture had clean, simple lines. The bed had a firm and supportive mattress and deliciously soft sheets. Blackout curtains blocked out the noise and light of the busy city.

The dark, quiet room and comfortable bed helped me sleep soundly. Waking up to beautiful colors and simple furniture made me feel calm and ready to explore the day. The Opus room inspired me to refresh my own master bedroom, which I painted a velvety navy blue and draped with autumn-orange silk curtains that block the light and frame the view of our garden. A restful room needn't be boring.

Once you've taken your staycation or visited beautiful rooms online, write down how your master bedroom feels now, how you would like it to feel, and what would need to change to generate that new feeling. Consider color, bed and nightstand size, comfort, temperature, and light and sound control.

What I learned from my sleep vacation:

_____

_____

_____

_____

_____

_____

Activity 15. Bedroom Eyes

It's time to look at your bedroom with new eyes. List all the items that are either 1) unrelated to sleep or sex, or 2) broken, shabby, or leftover from an old relationship. Eliminate at least three items that are unrelated to sleep or sex: toss, donate, or move them elsewhere in your house. Make a plan for repairing what is broken, and, if possible, immediately get rid of anything that evokes past relationships. (Note: I realize it's not always practical to get rid of an entire set of furniture leftover from a past relationship. At least toss the sheets—stat!—and replace them with the most luxurious sheets you can afford right now.)

Items that have nothing to do with sex or sleep:	Items in need of repair or replacement:	Items that are leftovers from an old relationship:
_____	_____	_____
_____	_____	_____
_____	_____	_____
_____	_____	_____

Activity 16. Put the "Om" in Home

No one but you (and your partner) can decide what kind of refuge you need in your bedroom. If you have a high-stress, high-intensity job (including child-rearing) you might need a spa-like, tranquil bedroom. If you have a low-key, even boring and under-stimulating job, you might want to infuse your bedroom with deep sensuality and passion. Your home, especially your bedroom, should be an oasis that meets *your* needs. As long as the end result is a space where you feel restored and where nothing is demanded of you, you will have been successful. Go to happystartsathome.com and try the free guided meditation to help you visualize your perfect, most supportive space. Once you have listened to the twenty-minute meditation, come back and journal on what you discovered during that quiet journey.

What I learned from the guided meditation:

_____
_____
_____
_____
_____
_____

TO SUM UP

The health benefits of good sleep cannot be overstated. With a good night's sleep you can do nearly anything. But when sleep deprived, even a well-mannered, mature grown-up becomes as irritable as a two-year-old in the middle of a tantrum. The great news is that you don't have to leave the quality of your sleep to chance. You can tune into the natural rhythms of your body by controlling the light and noise that comes into your room. You can dedicate your bedroom to rest and romance and banish the outside world. And you can clear your room of not only dust and debris but also old relationships and negative memories that would otherwise drag you down. By confidently changing your room to create a restful space, you can invite peace and tranquility into your life and prepare yourself to take on the world each new day!

Chapter 5.
Happy and in Love: Embracing Romance and Companionship

**"Let us always meet each other with a smile,
for the smile is the beginning of love."
—Mother Teresa**

THE DESIGN OF YOUR HOME CAN HELP keep your love life alive or even bring new love into your life. It can also keep love away. Design that sparks love isn't particularly magical or "woo-woo." It's not about love potions or painting your walls red. It's simply about becoming aware of the messages your home is sending out about how open you are to sharing your space and your life with another person.

If you want to bring love into your life, or rekindle an existing relationship, consider three basic needs:

1. Know yourself first.
2. Have space that is about *both* of you.
3. Allow room for change and growth.

LOVING AND KNOWING YOURSELF

**"You yourself, as much as anybody in the
entire universe, deserve your love and
affection." —Buddha**

Whether you are just starting out on the road of love, or you've been around the block a few times, you can't be an effective partner for anyone else if you haven't first figured out and embraced your own strength and worth. Your home actually reflects how well you know—and love—yourself.

Your home represents you. And just as a bird's nest would never be mistaken for a squirrel's nest, your home should be unique to you. Your home should help you say, "I know who I am, what I like, and what I want. I know where it is I am headed." If you don't establish this kind of home *before* you partner with someone else (particularly someone who *does* know what they want and has strong opinions about it), you may find yourself steamrolled by love and either never find your own voice, or one day feel the need to break free from the partnership just so you can sing your own song. Come into the relationship singing your own music and you both have a better chance at success. Shaping your home to fit you perfectly is a part of that journey.

In the years before you share a home with another person, you have a wonderful chance to create a unique, personal space without the vote or opinion of another person. Cherish this time. Often we are so eager to move from singlehood into partnership that we miss that wonderful chapter when all the choices are our own and there are no arguments over how to spend money and which paint color to choose.

If you are in-between partners, or newly single, take this wonderful opportunity to create a personal shelter. Don't settle for the way things have always been. Play with your home and see what fits the *new* you. Flex your creative muscles and see what feels right in this chapter of being single.

FINDING YOURSELF IN YOUR SPACE

> **"If we are comfortable with our homes,**
> **we are comfortable with ourselves."**
> **—Suzy Chiazzari**

Once your home reflects *you*, you'll start to feel a lot more settled about being on your own. You'll feel so much more at home in your house that the urgency to share your space will likely diminish. Watch out! This is the very moment in which you may get what you asked for.

For years my vivacious, beautiful client Hannah wanted to put down roots, get married, and start a family. She had a lot going for her: a successful career, a lovely apartment, and an active social life. Still, she hadn't met a partner with whom she could see herself establishing a long-term home.

When I walked into Hannah's apartment, I saw right away why she had called me: It *looked* like she'd just moved in, but she'd lived there for five years! Hannah admitted she was tired of living like she was waiting for Mr. Right to make it all come together. She figured that if she was going to live the single life, she might as well commit to it and love it.

We worked together to create a welcoming, feminine space that really felt like home to her. Hannah loved the space so much that she started not only spending more time there, but also inviting family and friends over more often. The result? Within a year, her increased social circle led her to both meet and marry the man of her dreams. Together they moved into the house of her dreams, too! Be careful what you ask for. You just might get it.

MAKING ROOM FOR LOVE

> **"Be ready for love when it does come.
> Prepare the field and be ready to
> nourish love. Be loving, and you will be
> lovable. Be open and receptive to love."**
> —Louise Hay, *You Can Heal Your Life*

Let's say you've done a great job of creating a space that reflects your preferences, desires, and dreams. If you're committed to bringing romantic love into your life, now it's time to make space for another person. This may feel a bit opposed to the effort you put into making your place your own, but it's not. You are not decorating as if someone else already lives there; you are simply creating a little room in your home and heart for someone else.

SENDING THE RIGHT MESSAGE

The home is like a beacon that signals to the world whether you are ready to give and receive love. This is true both when you are looking for love *and* when you are in an established relationship. Let's consider rooms I have seen that send exactly the opposite message.

Rooms that appear to reject romance:
- A single adult woman's bedroom with stuffed animals lining the windowsill and a pink satin comforter on the bed.

- A single guy's bedroom with a mattress on the floor and an old sheet tacked over the window.
- A woman's bedroom with a double bed pushed up against the wall, and both a large closet and two large dressers overflowing with clothes.
- A well-to-do bachelor's living room dressed to the nines in high-quality furnishings, all in heavy masculine black leather and sharp-edged stainless steel, focused on a massive flat-screen TV.
- A socialite's living room painted pale peach and furnished with a gorgeous white silk sofa, a cream wool rug, sheer linen curtains, and a glass coffee table.
- A couple's bedroom so full of kid's toys, paperwork, and laundry, you'd never know the room was meant for rest and sensuality.
- A man's "office" stuffed with unused belongings—old papers, discarded furniture, and shopping bags filled with returns that never made it back to the store.

Each of these clients insisted that they were open to love and ready to share their life and home with another person, yet their rooms all flashed a big "No Vacancy" sign. Stuffed animals and pink satin communicates a deeper connection to childhood than adulthood. A mattress on the floor and a sheet over a window suggests that the person living in that room isn't ready to commit to anything that requires thought or investment. A bed pushed against the wall literally blocks the way for another person to crawl into bed, and an overstuffed closet signals "no more room."

PREPARING FOR PARTNERSHIP

In *The Secret*, Marie Diamond recounts the story of a man who wanted to find a partner and get married, but he'd filled the walls of his home with paintings of women standing alone in poses that showed rejection of the viewer. "His wish [to be married] could not manifest. The outer level of himself—his house—was contradicting his wish all the time." Author Rhonda Byrne uses Diamond's story to remind readers that "when you want to attract something into your life, make sure your actions don't contradict your desires."

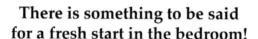

There is something to be said for a fresh start in the bedroom!

Pictures of old girlfriends, gifts from old boyfriends, and even mementos of childhood may need to be tucked away if you really are ready to begin an emotionally healthy relationship. Likewise I recommend changing up the wall color and splurging on new bedding if you are coming out of a relationship and want to find new love. There is something to be said for a fresh start in the bedroom! According to Byrne, "What you think about the most, or focus on the most, is what will appear in your life." If you're staring at your past, then you'll live in the past. Clear it out and make way for a bright and love-filled future. Goodwill is a great place for upcycling and clearing the Icky Stuff from your home.

MAKING ROOM FOR YOUR NEW PARTNER

> **"When you recover or discover something that nourishes your soul and brings joy, care enough about yourself to make room for it in your life."**
> **—Jean Shinoda Bolen**

It can be really hard to make room for a new person in your life after you've invested time and money to make your home fit you just right. That said, it's possible that your room is *too perfect*. Now that you've invited a new person into your home, your partner may be looking around your too-perfect room and wondering if there is any room for them. You might be naively content (*I have my perfect place and my perfect guy!*) but your partner might feel like a visitor, no matter how beautiful the space, because he's living in someone else's home. In *Our Place*, Suzy Chiazzari writes this:

> It is often difficult to move into another person's space, even if it belongs to a loving partner. The person who lives there will

inevitably have created his own little world. His home will be filled with the things he likes and the colors that please him, and he will have organized himself in the way that suits his lifestyle. Above all, he is likely to have established his own rituals, such as leaving the key in a certain place or doing the laundry at a particular time.

The newcomer is at a disadvantage, for there may not be space for all her belongings. The long-term occupant may feel put out as his routine will be disturbed. Both partners need to make compromises and to make room for each other.

Working through the activities in this book together, especially in Chapter 1, can open up a discussion for the two of you.

It's harder to modify an already existing space than to start over from scratch as a team. I worked with a very-much-in-love couple who really struggled as they started to co-habitate. Maria had recently moved into Anderson's ultramodern, utterly gorgeous home. He had designed the home from scratch with masculine, high-end finishes, a pan-Asian aesthetic, and large, in-your-face art pieces. Her shabby-chic style was about as far from Zen Modern as you could get. And while Maria appreciated that Anderson's home was fabulously and meticulously crafted, to her it felt cold and unfriendly. Fortunately for her, he was very willing to compromise. In the end they blended their unique styles, and the home became a beautiful testament to their love and what they were creating together.

GETTING ON THE SAME PAGE

It is so wonderful when partners recognize that they both need to feel at home in their new situation. It is much harder when one person is oblivious to the problem. Several of my female clients have moved into homes their new husbands once shared with their former wives. That happened to Jill when she married and moved in with Connor. Connor had already purchased furniture and could see no reason in the world why it should change. Not only had he been just as involved as his last wife in choosing the colors and furniture for his home but, to make matters worse, Connor's former wife, a woman he'd loved dearly, had passed away. Despite his love for Jill, Connor couldn't see that she felt like a visitor in her new home, haunted by the history of that past marriage. And because Connor's first wife had died, Jill felt like it would be too inconsiderate to ask him to redecorate the house.

In the case of another couple I worked with, the homeowner, Ray, had never particularly cared about wall colors or furniture choices. His ex-wife had selected most of them, and after they divorced he just left all the colors up on the walls and furniture in place. Like Connor, he felt that everything was fine the way it was. His new wife, Emily, on the other hand, hated the colors, not only because she thought they were ugly but also because they felt like leftovers from his old relationship. She'd lived in the house for years, trying to get used to it, but she hadn't felt "at home" for a single moment. Lucky for Emily, by the time they hired me, Ray was on board with making changes.

I encounter this kind of scenario over and over again. You finally find someone with whom you want to share your whole life. You move in and discover that your partner is either unwilling to change the space or unaware that change is necessary to turn "his house" into "our house." Your new partner, already established in the home, may not realize that without updates to the space, you actually feel trapped in someone else's house, particularly if the ex-spouse selected the colors and furnishings.

There are so many ways you and your partner can make blending homes a positive experience. Whether you are moving into your partner's home or inviting a new person to share your space, have a conversation. Try to speak without judgment (even when you're tempted to tell him his furniture is ugly) and you'll have a much smoother transition into cohabitation. Enlist the help of an interior design coach if you can't figure it out on your own.

MAKING ROOM FOR THE LOVE YOU ALREADY HAVE

**"Indifference and neglect often do much
more damage than outright dislike."
—J. K. Rowling**

Many couples start off great, but year by year one of the partners seems to get nudged out of the space, and romance is neglected. If women struggle more when they move into a partner's space, I find that men are more often squeezed out of their own homes.

When we commit to a partner, we commit to compromise and sharing—our feelings, our fears, our dreams, *and our sofa*. How we share our physical space can be a strong indicator of whether this is a partnership or a dictatorship. Your space reveals if you really are partners, or if you are more like housemates, sharing a space but not committed to compromise.

When we commit to a partner, we commit to compromise and sharing - our feelings, our fears, our dreams, *and* our sofa.

If your home is perfectly decorated but only represents *you*, consider what that says about your feelings toward your spouse and what that suggests to the world about his or her place in your home. Entire sitcom episodes mock towels that are only meant for decoration and recliners that are banished once a woman takes over, but the joke can quickly go from amusing to damaging. Have you unconsciously turned "our home" into "my home"?

Take the classic struggle over the ugly recliner: he loves it; you hate it. Sure the argument could be made that if he loves you, then he will let it go. But it's not always about you, or about having a perfectly decorated space. See if there is a way to replace it with something you both love, but realize that sometimes love means saying the chair gets to stay. Sometimes he just wants to feel it's his home too.

MAKING SPACE FOR MAKING LOVE

"A successful marriage requires falling in love many times, always with the same person." —Mignon McLaughlin

Perhaps you haven't taken over your home, but maybe Stuff has. Some homes have been so neglected that they no longer serve *anyone*. This tends to happen when a partner, or the marriage, gets taken for granted. The office that was meant for your spouse gets "borrowed temporarily" when you cleaned up "that one time." The little pile of stuff never quite left the office, and somehow it continued to grow. Before long the office became nothing more than a storeroom, and your partner no longer had a room for his or her own creativity and growth.

But wait! What's that you say? He wasn't *really* using the room that much? In fact, he actually helped move half that stuff into the room? It's okay: we're not placing blame here. No matter how it happened, the fact is that your spouse no longer has dedicated space.

NEGLECTING THE BEDROOM

Marriage neglect shows up in many rooms in the house, but most commonly it's the bedroom that tends to stagnate over the years. When we put energy into the house, we usually take care of the public spaces (kitchens, living rooms) first. Don't get me wrong: the public spaces *are* important. They define the family culture, create space for spending time together with family and friends, and help us feel secure and confident no matter what the world throws our way. But the bedroom is no less important, because that is where we tend to our marriage, where we stand together and repair what the world wore down that day. When our bedroom is more about the work we have to do than the love we need to make, when it is filled with toys from the kids, papers from work, and laundry that needs folding, we miss an opportunity to nurture our marriage. You must have a time and place where you are allowed to rest, laugh, and touch, without anything else demanding your time.

I've heard people say that the master bedroom doesn't matter that much because "all you do there is sleep." While that may be mostly true, a UCLA study documented in Jeanne Arnold's *Life at Home in the Twenty-First Century* showed that while soothing, spa-like master bedroom suites tend to be the least-used space in the home during waking hours, they do serve as retreats from the stress of clutter, housework, and raising a family. Arnold says the study found that "although they are underused, in one sense they conform to the ideal: whereas dense accumulations of objects invade other rooms of the house, we find that the [master] suites are kept relatively tidy and uncluttered, suggesting that these spaces are treated differently and hold some positive psychological significance for harried parents." It's a lot like meditating. You might only spend twenty minutes a day doing it, but just visiting that quiet space makes you feel calmer and helps you be more productive for the other twenty-three hours and forty minutes of the day.

EMBRACING EVOLUTION: LETTING LOVE GROW AND CHANGE

**"Change is the law of life. And those
who look only to the past or present are
certain to miss the future."
—John F. Kennedy**

One final note: A love-focused home permits change and growth. That means letting the people in the house evolve and explore over time. When you read Chapter 11, Happy and Creative: Playing at Any Age, you'll discover that you have permission to change, and that it is natural and normal for your preferences in food, hobbies, and other interests to shift as you go through life. Not only is it natural, it is encouraged. That which does not grow, dies.

If we give ourselves permission to change and grow, we must also allow growth in those we love. Unsurprisingly, many people feel resentful when their partners change the rules on them. It feels uncomfortable, especially if the new rule gets in the way of what *you* want. It can be as big as one person wanting a new career that requires moving across the country, or as small as someone wanting their coffee prepared in a new way.

My grandparents had a major falling out when my grandfather asked my grandmother to change his twenty-five-year habit of eating bacon and eggs for breakfast every morning to something "more healthy" like peanut butter on toast. My mother describes it as World War III. My grandmother took his request as an insult to her cooking, like she'd been doing it wrong all those years. By taking it personally, she let a small change in preference injure their long marriage. She couldn't let him change.

It's not always comfortable, but commitment requires flexibility and adapting to the evolution of your partner, just as you hope they will do for you.

Use the following exercises to explore your relationship with yourself, your space, and the love in your life.

Activity 17. Love Map: Yours vs. Mine

Create a basic floor plan of your home. It doesn't matter if it's to scale. Just be sure to represent each of the spaces, including closets and garages inside the house and decks and gardens outside. (Note: If you prefer, you can list the rooms instead of drawing a floor plan and then mark by each as directed below.)

If you do not live with a partner, first mark areas that feel like they perfectly represent *you* in one color, and mark areas that feel like they belong to someone else, or feel bland, in another color. Then go back through the space and mark areas that feel like they have open space for a partner, and mark areas that feel like they are too stuffed and do not leave space for a partner.

If you live with a partner, try to do this exercise with them. Both of you can use your own color and identify the rooms that feel like "you," the rooms that feel like "us," and the rooms that feel like "me." Then go back over the map and mark the areas that make it easy to talk or touch, and mark areas of the house that get in the way of talking or touching as a couple.

Look over the map. Any surprises? Are there areas that you thought were about "us" that your partner sees differently? Is there as much room for another person in your home as you expected? Is there enough of "you" in your home? Take a moment to journal on your experience, answering these questions: Is there a balance of space in my home for me, for my partner (either present or future), and for us together? Are there any lingering ghosts of past relationships in my space that need addressing?

_____

_____

_____

_____

_____

_____

Activity 18. Alarm Signals?

Just like a sneeze can indicate a virus in your body, the things in your house can point to disease in your home. Of course, sometimes a sneeze just means there is a little dust in the air, so remember that the following exercise is not meant to create problems where none exist. Rather, this activity is designed to help you see your home for what it is and what it says and make changes if you need to. Check the boxes that are true for your home. For each box that you mark, read through the possible diagnoses. Feel free to refute it, add to it, or offer an explanation that feels more suited to your particular situation.

- ☐ **A dirty, permanently cluttered home:** may indicate messy past or present relationships, a lack of personal boundaries, or a feeling of vulnerability
- ☐ **Dreary colors and worn furnishings:** may indicate a fading relationship, depression, a feeling of lack or neglect
- ☐ **A stuffy atmosphere:** may indicate people who are bored with each other, strict control
- ☐ **Only one person's stuff represented:** may indicate an unequal partnership
- ☐ **Minimal, sparse style:** may indicate tight controls on your relationship, may also indicate an overwhelming work or personal life
- ☐ **Uncomfortable furniture:** may indicate a formal, uncomfortable relationship
- ☐ **No photos of you as a couple:** may indicate a casual relationship or lack of commitment
- ☐ **Unfinished decorating project:** may indicate a problem with commitment or decision-making
- ☐ **Too many belongings:** may indicate an inability to filter or establish boundaries
- ☐ **Dust on all the belongings:** may indicate a neglected home and relationships
- ☐ **Bare walls:** may indicate a lack of commitment to this place, this life, these relationships
- ☐ **Broken things:** may indicate low self-esteem and feeling of lack
- ☐ **Still-unpacked boxes:** may indicate a lack of commitment to this place, this life, these relationships
- ☐ **Inherited paint colors, especially from ex-lovers:** may indicate an inability to move on from the past, and a lack of self-identification within the home and relationship
- ☐ **Dirty walls:** may indicate a low self-esteem and feeling of lack
- ☐ **Museum-perfect spaces:** may indicate a formal, uncomfortable relationship
- ☐ **Offices that have become storage rooms:** may indicate an inability to filter or establish boundaries, also a fear of failure
- ☐ **Naked bedrooms:** may indicate a neglected romantic life or poor sex life, or a casual, non-committed relationship

- ☐ **Rooms overrun with kids' toys:** may indicate an inability to filter or establish boundaries
- ☐ **Dangerous furniture (such as glass-cornered coffee tables):** may indicate a formal, uncomfortable relationship, or rigidity

Thoughts? What came up for you here?

_____

_____

_____

_____

_____

_____

Activity 19. Setting the Stage for Love, Or Rekindling a Flame

Are you committed to love and to having a loving relationship in your home? If I were to look in your home, *would I believe you*? Check the box for each item you've got covered:

- ☐ I have a bed that is comfortable for two, with two generous nightstands and two easy-to-use, sturdy lamps on either side.
- ☐ My bedroom is clearly a room for adults, not for children or animals.
- ☐ My bedroom is a room for rest and romance. It is clear of laundry, paperwork, and other distractions from rest and romance.
- ☐ My closet and dresser have open space; everything in my closet and dresser fits; and nothing reminds me of my ex or past life.
- ☐ My living room has a space that feels comfortable and safe for spending time with another person.
- ☐ My entryway is clear of clutter; there is space for visitors to put down their belongings and stay awhile.
- ☐ It is easy to shut out the noise and light from the world when I want to retreat into my bedroom and rest or connect with my partner.
- ☐ My home clearly reflects who I am but is also flexible and ready for change.
- ☐ There are clean towels, fresh soap, and plenty of toilet paper in the bathroom.
- ☐ My home is easy to find from the street, with clearly marked house numbers and a safe walkway.

TO SUM UP

If you've been reaching for love for years but it remains out of your grasp, take a look around you. Do the messages in your home line up with what you say you want? If your love is feeling stale, eliminate love landmines and turn your home into a place where you can fall in love each day. If love has been elusive, create space in your home that invites newness and adventure into your life, and prepare a spot for your future lover. Set a table for two in your life, and invite love in.

Chapter 6.
Happy with Friends:
Creating Spaces for Gathering

"The world is round so that
friendship may encircle it."
—Pierre Teilhard de Chardin

IN TODAY'S WORLD WE TEND to be oversocialized yet underconnected. We have hundreds of online "friends," but many of us feel that we lack close friendships, people who love you enough to give up a weekend to help you move or stop by for a slow cup of tea. If you are lacking a rich social life and meaningful friendships, and wish to have more connection in your life, your home can help.

A space that invites, rather than prevents, relationship building should look presentable enough for you not to feel embarrassed by it. It should feel comfortable enough to linger in. It should feel so much like "you" that when you leave the house to go out and socialize, you have a clear, unshakable sense of who you are. And it should make you feel safe and secure.

No one likes to feel ashamed of where they live. At the same time, we are all bombarded by messages in magazines and on TV about how we should live and what our homes should look like. When they don't measure up we feel embarrassed and we apologize. But I say save your "sorry" for when it matters.

Not getting the living room vacuumed isn't a sin, and not having the guest room look like a perfect bed-and-breakfast isn't an insult to your guests. What *is* a problem is the shame that you feel. Why? Because shame puts a barrier between you and your visitor. You try to pay attention to your guest, but part of your mind is fixated on the cobwebs on the lamp and the cat hair on the chair. That kind of embarrassment keeps many people from having guests over at all. They put off inviting people over until the house is "better," "cleaner," or "done." Let's acknowledge that a house is never "done." It is as organic as we are, always shifting and adapting. Any space that isn't evolving is stagnant, a museum. That said, it *is* important that you get it to a place where it helps you build a fulfilling social life.

EMPTINESS AS AN OBSTACLE

Some people avoid inviting friends over to their home because the space isn't decorated—it feels cold, empty, and uninviting. One of my clients spent nearly a dozen years hating her living room. She hardly ever invited anyone over, not even her own sister. Finally, when her daughter moved out of the house and she went from single mom to empty nester, she gave herself permission to put energy and money into her living room. We didn't do anything more drastic than paint the walls a warm, inviting green, repaint the brick fireplace, and bring in comfortable furniture scaled properly for the space. But the room went from cold, unfriendly, and uninviting to warm, cozy, and personal. And she went from feeling embarrassed to hospitable. Better yet, even when sitting alone in her new empty-nest living room, she felt happy. She said it felt like "her."

Another client, a beautiful young woman in her late twenties, went through a major life shift when she divorced. She bought a condo, excited to launch her life as a newly single person. But soon after, she found herself stuck in a cold white-walled box with a beige couch and metal mini-blinds on the windows—not at all the new life she imagined for herself. Not only did she feel disinclined to make new friends and invite them over, but she also hardly wanted to be in the new place herself. This home was in no condition to support her goal of starting over romantically or socially. She reached out for help, and together we used color and accessories to transform the space into one that felt alive, youthful, and ready for adventure. In no time she found herself making new friends and inviting them to hang out at her place. We hadn't changed her social skills; we just eliminated an obstacle standing in the way of her goals.

ABUNDANCE AS AN OBSTACLE (OR, THE CURSE OF CLUTTER)

Your home can also prevent you from entertaining when you are embarrassed not by its emptiness, but by its clutter. Clutter seems to breed clutter, and before you know it, you can be neck deep. We all have different sensitivities to clutter, and it doesn't really matter if you've accumulated a few mail piles or reached true hoarder status. At whatever level, if clutter is making you feel ashamed or keeping you from having meaningful relationships, it's a problem.

There are many books on cutting clutter, and a lot of people who can help. When I personally work with clients to eliminate clutter, I make it pretty clear that I am not there to be an "organizer"; I am there to help lighten the load. Just labeling the clutter and moving it around will rarely create long-term change in the house—it requires letting go.

Just organizing clutter rarely creates long term change in a home - it requires letting go of some of the Stuff.

Creating a clutter-free, more inviting home can produce surprising results. One of my clients, James, had been laid off and suffered from depression. His wife, Leslie, tried to cheer James up by surprising him with a big-screen TV. Once the TV was installed in the living room, however, it became a huge eyesore. Leslie called me to integrate it into their tiny bungalow living room. As soon as I arrived, I could see that the main problem wasn't the TV: it was the overabundance of furniture. The space overflowed with the furnishings of *two* living rooms and sagged under all that weight.

Together we decluttered and donated carloads of stuff, rearranged the room to make the most of the remaining furniture and the big TV, and, of course, painted the room a cohesive color to tie it all together. It turned out that this basic makeover helped James emerge from the fog of his depression. Later he told me that he had felt lousy about the house, and it just added insult to injury to be both unemployed *and* embarrassed by his home—two signs of his "failure." The transformed living room looked like it belonged to someone successful and made James feel like he could have friends over and be proud of the space. In turn, welcoming friends into their home helped both James and Leslie rekindle social connections, an important part of battling depression. And having a functional office space allowed him to pursue his craft and ultimately start his own architectural drafting company, the best eliminator of his situationally-induced depression. Beautiful!

FACING SHAME HEAD ON

"The ornament of a house is the friends who frequent it." —Ralph Waldo Emerson

If you say you're embarrassed by your home and want to change it so you can invite friends over, but you resist making changes, you might want to dig a little more deeply and ask yourself if you really do want to create solid friendships. Houses gain weight the same way people do, and sometimes it happens because we are creating an unconscious barrier to protect ourselves from getting hurt. We *say* we want to invite friends over, but we avoid making the changes that will let that happen. We use the house as an excuse, because it is safer to stay behind our walls, protected within our fortress, in a place where we can't actually be hurt.

BRINGING COZY BACK (OR, HOW TO ACTUALLY DECORATE AN INVITING LIVING ROOM)

Assuming you don't really want to hide behind your walls, how can you create a home that feels natural and comfortable? Another client, Allie, owned a fabulous home with one of the most playful living rooms I'd ever seen. A tomato orange fireplace; sleek gray, low-profile midcentury couches . . . it just felt like a party. Still, she was frustrated because *no one* ever used it, not even her, and she really wanted a space where she and her friends could, and more importantly *would*, hang out. As we evaluated what to change, we figured out that her very tailored, stiff couches, lined up like benches, forced guests to face each other, almost as a direct challenge. And two square metal coffee tables were set diagonally so that sharp points angled toward the couches. Everything in the room was fun shaped and colorful, but not a thing in the room was inviting or friendly.

Once we identified why the room felt so unfriendly, Allie and I used the following design guidelines to reinvent the space and create an inviting living room. You can use them too:

1. **Invite comfortable conversation through the seating arrangement.** It should allow people to sit facing each other, side by side, or at 90 degrees to each other, depending on what feels right at the moment. Think of a fire pit, the feeling of folks gathered around a campfire. Avoid having the furniture all lined up like a hallway or a waiting room, or all facing a big TV.

2. **Create easy movement and flow.** Make it simple to enter and exit the room, ideally by two paths or at least a generous space. Leave at least thirty-six inches between pieces of furniture or walls that create a "hallway" or path. Avoid sharp angles intruding into the paths, and use round coffee tables when needed to create flow.

3. **Keep it human-scaled.** Avoid giant pieces of artwork towering over the room cathedral-style, and consider softening huge picture windows with simple drapes that gently frame the window. As much as possible, create nooks for intimacy—like quiet conversation and reading.

4. **Make it touchable.** Make generous use of soft throw pillows and blankets. Avoid anything that is unpleasant to touch or feels too delicate and off-limits to touch. Use feather or feather-like pillow inserts so they mold to your body instead of bouncing you off the sofa.

5. **Make it approachable.** If your guests feel like they have to be too careful, they'll never be at ease. Avoid a lot of glass, white fabric, shiny metal, or delicate objects of art.

6. **Light it up.** Layer the light by combining overhead lights with floor and table lamps. Adjust lighting based on the activity in the room: Brighter light makes your older guests more comfortable; lamplight is warmer, easier to control, and more flattering for everyone. Avoid having your only light source come from overhead or recessed lighting, because overhead lights cast deep shadows under the eyes. When people feel attractive, they are naturally more at ease.

7. **Consciously choose your wall colors.** Bright orange may be fun, but a sharp tangerine might be a little too forceful in its playfulness, practically screaming at your guests to have fun. A spiced pumpkin like Benjamin Moore's Buttered Yam might be a better choice. Or paint the walls a neutral color and bring in fabulous orange accessories.

When we applied these principles to Allie's living room, she ended up with a fun *and* friendly room, a place where we all wanted to linger just a little longer.

FEELING "AT HOME" MAKES IT EASIER TO MAKE FRIENDS

"It's like everyone tells a story about themselves inside their own head. Always. All the time. That story makes you what you are. We build ourselves out of that story." —Patrick Rothfuss

Having a home you feel proud of affects your social life at every age. I was so lucky as a child to have a house that always felt like home. What makes that remarkable is that my family moved around a lot because my dad was in the Army. Despite moving to one new place after another, my parents, especially my stepmom, Linda, gave me a secret weapon that I could use to make new friends wherever I went. Linda always had our home *done* by the time school started. When I say done, I mean she laid pretty area rugs on the floors, tucked welcome signs by the front door, hung curtains, positioned art on the walls, and decorated mine and my brothers' rooms so they felt homey. Our address might have changed, but it always felt like home every bit as much as the previous house. I felt secure knowing that my home was stable, felt proud to bring friends there, and as a result made friends more easily. It made all the difference.

Just like the way a feeling of safety and permanence affects our health (see Chapter 3), the feeling of permanence and belonging affects our desire and ability to form friendships. We are naturally more willing to connect when we know we are staying put. Conversely, when we live half-moved-in, half-unpacked, we increase our isolation. By putting down visual roots, we not only create a place to welcome friends but also feel more rooted and willing to invest in relationships.

HOME AWAY FROM HOME

Of course, not all socializing happens at home, but even when you go out your home supports or sabotages your efforts to create deep connections in your life. Your home should feel so "you" that when you go to networking or social events, you carry a crystal-clear sense of self.

A couple of years ago one of my clients found herself struggling with her sense of identity, confused about what she wanted from her friends or her business. Grace had recently cut ties with some destructive people in her life. For years Grace had defined herself in opposition to those hurtful people, and so she always had something concrete to fight against. And yet taking the (very healthy) step of walking away had left her feeling rootless and uncertain. This showed up in how she approached furnishing her home. It was temporary. It was "good enough." But it was also unpleasant, uncomfortable, and embarrassing.

As we worked together, Grace started moving things around and out of her home. She started giving it a chance to love her and support her. As she did that, she started giving herself a chance to be loved and supported by places, people, and circumstances that were not hurtful. Grace started to learn to trust others and, more importantly, to trust herself. She once remarked, "Last week it really hit me that my home is my consciousness . . . my consciousness is my home. Thinking about my home like this was like opening up this new idea of me, and then by making the changes and creating my new office I physically stepped into my new reality."

**We wake up every morning and
go to sleep every night in our home.
It cannot help but affect how we
engage with the world around us.**

Our homes, both literally and figuratively, shape our place in the world. It's where we wake every morning and go to sleep every night. It cannot help but affect how we engage with the world around us. If you are feeling oversocialized but underconnected and want to use your home as a way to fix that, consider hosting a book, wine, or garden club. A regular meeting, once a month, of a few like-minded people over the course of months or years can build genuine friendships and social bonds that are not replicated anywhere else in life! If you can't imagine inviting people into your home, either because you are stopped by emptiness or by clutter, make some changes as soon as you can!

LETTING PEOPLE IN

> **"Surround yourself with only people who**
> **are going to lift you higher."**
> **—Oprah Winfrey**

Lastly, remember that you can bring the right people into your life and keep the wrong people out. Revisit the safety checklist (Activity 10 in Chapter 3) and make sure that you are being intentional about whom you let in, both literally and figuratively. Your home must make you feel safe and secure, and who you keep out is every bit as important as who you welcome in.

Activity 20. Private vs. Public Spaces: Map Your Home's Social Life

Create a basic floor plan of your home. It doesn't have to be to scale, just make sure each space is represented, including outside decks and gardens. Choose three colored pencils or crayons.

Once you have drafted your floor plan, use one color to mark areas that are considered social spaces and are comfortably used by three or more people. Use a different color to mark areas that are considered personal and private, just meant for one or two people. Use a third color to mark areas that feel uninviting and unfriendly, places that aren't being effectively used regardless of whether they are meant for social or private use.

Look over your colored floor plan. Are you surprised by which areas feel private or intimate, which areas feel social, and which areas feel uninviting? Take a moment to write about your experience in mapping the social life in your home:

_____

_____

_____

_____

_____

_____

Activity 21. Making Friends

Let's assess your social life. Remember that there are no right or wrong answers, and your preferences may differ from others in your family. Maybe you draw energy from quiet moments relaxing on your own. Perhaps you love a good party, but only occasionally. A "good" social life might involve hundreds of people, or just a few close friends. The only cue to follow is your personal contentment level. But if you feel you are lacking in the social and friendship departments, take that as a sign to create change and evaluate how your home can help. If you are content and feel fulfilled in your relationships, don't feel you "should" change anything!

Complete the following phrases:
- The last time I had friends over was _____ and it made me feel _____
- The last time I apologized to someone for the state of my home was _____ and it was because _____
- If friends were to drop by right now, I would feel _____
- If my boss were to drop by right now I would feel _____

Based on your answers, take a moment to journal on the status of your social life and changes you would like to see in it:

_____
_____
_____
_____
_____
_____

Activity 22. Taking Action

Now that you've read this chapter, what three changes would you like to make in your friendships and social life? What resources do you need to make those changes occur? By what date could those changes happen? What small, tangible step can you take to make progress today?

A change: _____
Date this will happen by (both a date I'd like and that is achievable): _____
Resources I need: _____
A step I can take today: _____

A change: _____

Date this will happen by (both a date I'd like and that is achievable): _____

Resources I need: _____

A step I can take today: _____

A change: _____

Date this will happen by (both a date I'd like and that is achievable): _____

Resources I need: _____

A step I can take today: _____

TO SUM UP

If I had a dollar for every time I heard someone apologize for the state of his or her home, I'd be one rich gal. If you feel embarrassed by your home to the point where you rarely welcome friends into your space, figure out what needs to change (including your expectations, the physical space, or both) and make those changes so you feel free to nurture your friendships both in and outside of your home.

We can't help but be impacted by the status and style of our homes: there are simply too many home improvement shows and decorating magazines linking our nests to our social standing. But while we can't disconnect our social comfort from our space, we can become conscious of the link and create spaces that connect us to the world on a more meaningful level.

Chapter 7.
Happy with Family:
Building a Family Identity

*"In every conceivable manner, the family
is link to our past, bridge to our future."*
—Alex Haley

OUR HOMES, OUR *NESTS*, ARE PHYSICAL REPRESENTATIONS of our family identities. What we choose to have around us says who we are, or at least how we wish to be perceived. From the American flag and basketball hoop out front, to the chicken coop and raised garden out back, our homes both *tell* the story of our families and *reinforce* that story.

The design and decoration of your home doesn't just reflect your family narrative, it also profoundly impacts your family life. What you have, or do not have, in your home affects how you play and work together. How you set up your furniture affects where and how you eat as a family, how you spend your time together as a family, and how you identify both as part of, and independently from, your family. What I mean is that the things in your home not only result from who you are, but also affect who you will become. That means you control the direction of your story. You are not only living it; you are writing it.

**The things you keep in your home
not only represent who you are, they
also affect who you will become.**

When I think back to my childhood home, I remember the antique Winchester rifle that hung over our couch. My dad would just give it a nod when my dates picked me up, setting an expectation of how his daughter would be treated. Would he have used it? Unlikely. Did it send a clear message to my boyfriends? Yep. I also think of the "cleaning closet" with the broom and vacuum that came out every evening when my brothers and I did the after-dinner chores, teaching us that we were contributing members of the family. Not a single evening passed when we didn't work together to keep the house tidy. I also remember the glass display shelves full of Hummel figurines, which reminded us to be careful in a grown-up space. These items were like friends to me, because they were familiar and helped me know I was home.

Our tidy home was decorated with pretty pictures and pillow shams that matched the bed comforters, but I wouldn't have called it high-end. A pleasant home needn't be expensively appointed. In many ways it is better if it isn't. I now share a home with my new husband, who is a talented remodeling contractor—and also a *bit* of a bull in a china shop. I knew early on that when I put our home together, I needed to do it with objects and furnishings that were relatively indestructible, or at least easily replaceable. We opted for Ikea dishes and consignment-store living room furniture, and I staged my cherished objets d'art on the mantle. We managed to create a home that is both beautiful and comfortable. Everything is "allowed" to be used, and nothing requires overly careful handling. I never want to have an *American Beauty* moment like when Lester Burnham, portrayed by film actor Kevin Spacey, attempts to make love to his wife, Carolyn, and she stops him by saying, "This is a four-thousand-dollar sofa, upholstered in Italian silk. It's *not* just a couch." Ouch. Why doom a marriage with a fabric choice? I hope you never find yourself safeguarding your sofa instead of being intimate with your spouse.

VALUES-DRIVEN DESIGN

I am sure we can agree that a comfortable, family-focused home doesn't need to be expensively appointed, but what *are* the keys to creating a safe, cozy, inviting home? Start by identifying your family's values and culture, and then build an environment that supports those values. No one can tell you what your values should be, but once you have identified them, it becomes easy to design around them. Here are examples of some of my clients' values and corresponding design ideas that serve those values:

Value: Spending time outdoors, hiking in the woods, playing outside.
Design: A mudroom with an outdoor entry; easy-to-access storage for outerwear such as boots, gloves, and hats; and easy-to-clean flooring.

Value: Eating together, praying at meals, sharing the day over lovingly prepared food.
Design: A dedicated dining room that is casual and inviting, free from electronic distractions, and close to the kitchen so that setting up and cleaning up create more opportunities for family interaction.

Value: Hosting parties for your community or networking group.
Design: An open-concept kitchen that invites relaxed interaction between the cook and guests, and has easy-to-care-for flooring that is forgiving when it comes to cleaning up bits and crumbs after the party.

Value: Multigenerational living.
Design: A home with spaces that can be personalized for each generation so that no one feels like they are living in someone else's home, are accessible and safe with generous lighting and few steps, and promote both gathering and privacy when needed.

Value: Having conversations.
Design: A living room with furniture that's arranged for easy conversation rather than focused on the TV; adjustable lighting that works for different activities like reading, playing games, or relaxing with a cup of cocoa or a glass of wine; comfortable, easy-to-maintain seating that's free from dog slobber, cat hair, Cheerios, and flat cushions.

DON'T SET YOURSELF UP FOR FRUSTRATION AND FAILURE

The best way to maintain your home and your sanity is to understand your family culture and work *with* the habits of the people living in and visiting your home. If you have a rambunctious family with teens and dogs constantly coming in and out, installing white wool carpeting will just invite disaster. If you regularly host foodie parties and guests wander your home holding plates of red sauce and glasses of red wine, reconsider that $10,000 silk and wool rug. If you really prefer gardening over dusting, think twice before you install glass shelves to display your grandmother's figurine collection. Design with your family and lifestyle in mind, and create peace.

PERSONALIZING YOUR PLACE

If you're new to decorating, you're unlikely to achieve a developed, rich, personal feeling on your first try. Even if you hire a designer to accessorize with delightful, whimsical treasures, it still won't feel as warm and personal as it will when you collect items over time. It's great to finish the house enough that it feels done, but think of some elements as placeholders, and then let yourself play over the years. Eventually you'll bring home a fabulous oil painting from your trip to Italy or the Grand Canyon and replace that placeholder print. Collect a bag full of seashells from your day at the beach, pour out the generic ornaments that your decorator put in the glass jar on your mantle, and refill it with the shells that now tell a story in your life.

If you're a seasoned decorator, take a walk through your home and explore the stories that are already present. Visit each room and think carefully about how each object makes you feel. Some will evoke pleasant, positive memories; others will bring up guilt, frustration, even shame, fear, or sadness. Others maybe "should" be meaningful but really are no longer important to you. As you go through your space, you'll probably associate stories with each item you see—some happy, some sad, some bittersweet. Of course, just because an item has a story doesn't mean you're stuck with it or have to keep telling yourself that story. If it's time to move on, do so! And if it's someone else's burden or debt or shame you are keeping in your home through that object, let it go. It was never yours to begin with.

HONORING THE PAST, EMBRACING THE FUTURE: THE KEEPERS

How we handle the stuff in our houses creates an important lesson for us—and for our kids. Some people keep everything and end up with a house stuffed so full that nothing has meaning. Overstuffed homes can be suffocating to the point of embarrassment for everyone who lives there. Guests might not be invited over or, if they are, apologies are made for the state of the house. Every interaction is tinged with shame.

Filled-to-the-brim homes are not only embarrassing, they can be a bit haunted, too. When you keep everything, there are three unintended consequences.

First, the bad stuff stays. The bedding you shared with your ex-wife is still slept in. The nightgown that old boyfriend gave you still hangs in the closet. The favorite vase your sister chipped when she was helping clean up after your mom's memorial service—it not only reminds you that you're still mad at her for being so careless but also keeps you stuck in the grief of losing your mom.

Second, the past is never permitted to go away. How can your daughter feel she is free to explore being a teenager if her room is perpetually stuck in seven-year-old status and the fridge is covered in her kindergarten artwork? How can you improve as an artist when your work from a decade ago still crowds your studio?

Last of all, there isn't room for anything new. Sure, you could bring in a beautiful new lounge chair, but where the heck would it go? Crammed next to the ratty recliner and shredded cat tree? As good parents and as good caretakers of ourselves, we have to know when to let go of the old and make room for the new.

HONORING THE PAST, EMBRACING THE FUTURE: THE ELIMINATORS

While some folks keep everything, others are so brutal about getting rid of things, or about keeping out anything that doesn't "match" the house, that nothing is ever permitted to grow in meaning. Who can be at ease in sterile perfection? It's an uncomfortable way to live, and creates an environment where everyone must be constantly alert and careful. Heaven forbid something got damaged!

My grandmother's house was one of those perfectly curated spaces. White wool area rugs, glass display shelves, and antiques everywhere. I remember in vivid detail the day my cousin and I were sliding down the stairs on our bellies, unbeknownst to my grandmother, and we knocked over and broke a candle on the landing. I really and truly thought she would kill us. Obviously no murders took place, but the stress and fear that such a too-perfect environment created had a severe and lasting impact on how we behaved, for better or worse.

A too-spotless, perfectly clean home can make people feel uneasy.

A perfectly curated home can be just as distressing as a too-cluttered home. In a too-cluttered home, nothing has meaning because there is too much stuff. In a too-sparse home, things of value may be edited out and meaning isn't allowed to develop. Spaces stay generic, no matter how beautiful they are, rather like a hotel room. Those who live there never really feel at home. This *passing-through* existence can lead to a difficulty in setting down roots, forming long-term relationships, and building trust with new people. This comes up especially often for people who frequently move from place to place and perpetually feel like transient guests.

While it's important to remove things that aren't serving you, it is just as important to hold on to things that are meaningful, and let each person in the home help create that meaning. That might require giving everyone their own space to control. Or perhaps developing a family vision and then decorating in harmony with that vision. Although many architectural magazines depict the minimalist home as the most elevated, ideal way of living, in reality a sterile gallery-style house rarely makes a home. For that matter, even a too-spotless, perfectly clean home can make people feel uneasy. It's stifling. No one feels comfortable, the hostess has to work too hard, and the guests have to be too careful. There is such a thing as a too-perfect house.

BE CHOOSY: WHEN BLESSINGS ARE A BURDEN

> "I realize there's something incredibly
> honest about trees in winter, how they're
> experts at letting things go."
> —Jeffrey McDaniel

Blood may be thicker than water, but that doesn't mean you have to hold on to all your family heirlooms. My colleague, home organizer Stacy Erickson, reminds her clients that each of us has both the right and the responsibility to decide what comes into our lives. We get a say in who is in our life, what is in our home, and how we will be treated in this world. She explains that it is okay to say *no* when someone offers you a hand-me-down. People with very good intentions may decide that since you are just starting out you really should have their old furniture, but if you don't need another sofa, then you are inheriting a burden, not a gift.

Your extended family may think you should have your grandmother's rocking chair or the crib from your cousin just in case you get pregnant—you know, since you just got married. They may be well intentioned, but *you* are the one who determines what comes into your home and life, what gets to stay, and what needs to leave. Even if you were gifted with a bunch of family stuff years ago, you can still let your family know you'll be letting stuff go. Give them a date by which it will be leaving your home. If it's important enough to them, they'll take it. If it's not, then it can go to a family who will love it. Why hold on to something you dislike when someone out there could really and truly use it?

The lessons these choices teach, especially if you involve your kids in the process, can resonate over the years in many ways. It will show up in the daughter who leaves the employer who doesn't value her talents, and in the son who breaks up with the long-term girlfriend who treats him horribly. It will show up in the sister who finally understands that your home is full, and when she redecorates she finds a charity eager to accept her old stuff. The choices you make about what you will allow in your life and what must go will leave an impression on everyone around you. Meanwhile, your home becomes a place with a balance of history and opportunity, free of the ghosts of past pain, and ripe for growth and new adventures with your family.

Take a few minutes to think about your home as it relates to your family, and create intention behind how you set up your nest.

Activity 23. Family Map: Navigating the Family Home

Create a basic floor plan of your home. It doesn't need to be to scale. Just be sure that each space is represented, including inside storage, like closets and garages, and outside spaces like decks and gardens.

You can do this exercise on your own, but it's even better to complete it with at least one other family member. Let each family participant mark on the plan places that feel like family space, spaces that feel like they belong to a specific person, spaces that seem comfortable and fun, and spaces that feel off-limits. Use a different color for each of the four categories so that it's easy to see patterns after everyone has taken their turn. For example, if off-limits areas are marked in black, you'll easily see how everyone responds to a given room if it has a lot of black marks.

When everyone is finished, look over the map. Talk about what makes each space feel a given way. Maybe a room you thought of as communal has been taken over by one family member because that's where he always plays video games with his friends. Maybe another room feels uninviting because people keep bruising their shins on that darn glass coffee table. Once you have this information, decide what needs to change or be rebalanced. Jot the results here:

_____

_____

_____

_____

_____

_____

Activity 24. House Guests: Invited or Uninvited?

In this exercise you will visit with the "people" in your home. Choose a room and list at least a dozen items in that room. Include a variety: big furniture pieces, small decorative elements, even clutter like piles of junk mail. By each item on the list, write the name of a person or persons you associate with it: who made it, who gave it to you, who it was meant for, or some other association. When you've completed your list, ask yourself, are there people in that room who shouldn't be there? Are there too many voices? Too few?

	Item	People linked with the item
1.		
2.		
3.		
4.		
5.		
6.		
7.		
8.		
9.		
10.		
11.		
12.		

Activity 25. Family Values

In this exercise you will consciously inventory your family's values. Remember that every family is different, and no one can determine these for you. What is important is to identify what you value, and use that as a guide as you set up your home. By allowing your values to guide your choices, you will reinforce your family culture, make sure that your life, activities, and values are aligned, and create a stable, trustworthy environment.

List your personal or family values and identify at least three objects or spaces that represent each value. If one or more of your values is *not* represented, make the changes you need to get it represented. As an example, I love to throw parties and want everyone to feel at ease; I never want them to feel they have to be too careful. You might say I value "comfort" and "indestructibility." Three things that represent those values in my home are: inexpensive Ikea dishes that are easily replaced, a sofa that is high quality but secondhand, and easy-to-clean wood floors.

To help get you started, I've included an example of my values list.

Rebecca's personal and family values:

Comfort	Intelligence	Independence
Warmth	Travel	Simplicity
Creativity	Nature and time outside	Affordability
Playfulness	Cleanliness	Happiness

Now it's your turn:

Value: Three items or spaces that support and reflect that value:

_____   _____ _____   _____

_____   _____ _____   _____

_____   _____ _____   _____

_____   _____ _____   _____

_____   _____ _____   _____

Activity 26. Taking the Temperature

In this exercise you will explore the emotions that run through each room. Does a lot of arguing happen here? Eating or overeating? Sleeping or not sleeping? Work or procrastination? Laughing or crying? List each room of your home and identify three emotions that are regularly present in each room. Then list who is involved in that emotion:

Room	Emotional activities	People linked with the emotional activity
_____	_____	_____
	_____	_____
	_____	_____
_____	_____	_____
	_____	_____
	_____	_____
_____	_____	_____
	_____	_____
	_____	_____
_____	_____	_____
	_____	_____
	_____	_____
_____	_____	_____
	_____	_____
	_____	_____
_____	_____	_____
	_____	_____
	_____	_____
_____	_____	_____
	_____	_____
	_____	_____

After you check in with your spaces, consider if the reality runs counter to what you desire for your life and family. Perhaps adjusting the furniture layout would create a less confrontational space. Maybe it is time to give the teens more privacy. Maybe removing paperwork, piles of laundry, and kids' toys from the bedroom will induce tranquility and better sleep.

TO SUM UP

As you create a space for your family, know that your home's design and layout will impact how you spend your time together, how you grow and change over time, and the lessons that your kids take away from their childhood.

Designing for the family should be both values-driven *and* reality-driven. A focus on values ensures that your home will support your family's activities and allows you to figure out what you really need from your home. Do you need areas to play games, share a meal, watch TV, talk, work on chores together, do homework? In today's world it is unlikely that each family member will be doing the same thing at the same time, but it can be enough to be sharing the same space, with each person able to do what brings him or her joy. Meanwhile, designing with reality in mind ensures that you work *with* the habits, activities, and ages of those in your home, instead of creating opportunity for conflict that could have been avoided.

Your family will grow and change over time as each person transitions through the chapters of life and invites in new children, new spouses, and new physical needs. Allow your house to keep up with the changing times by letting go of what worked last decade and making room for new adventures.

Chapter 8.
Happy with the Kids: Raising Confident, Competent Children

"The greatest gifts you can give your children are the roots of responsibility and the wings of independence."
—Denis Waitley

PARENTS KNOW HOW QUICKLY TIME PASSES BY. No matter how much you want to freeze time, children grow up fast. In this chapter we'll talk about how you can make the most of your time with your kids, helping create lasting memories while teaching valuable lessons along the way.

My mom was a master of teaching practical lessons in a really fun way. When I was about twelve, she taught me about money and independence by giving me a day to shop with her anywhere in San Francisco. The catch? I was in charge of all the transportation. I had to map out our routes, figure out time-tables, buy the tickets, and pay the vendors. We used the subway, we walked, we took a taxi, we rode the trolley. We had great fun, shopped all day, and along the way I learned about planning, budgeting, tipping, and navigation.

The family home is a wonderful vehicle for these kinds of life lessons. If your goal is to raise a capable, intelligent adult, look to your home for teaching about budgeting, consequences, and empowerment.

TEACH ABOUT BUDGETING

So your teen is itching to make over her room. Take this opportunity to teach a lesson in budgeting! Start by setting parameters: what you will allow, what you can afford, and whether your teen will have to contribute her own money to the project. No matter what limits you set, if you say yes to this project, you have a wonderful chance to teach your teen about planning and spending wisely. If your teen is particularly responsible, consider getting a prepaid Visa card with a set dollar amount. Before she makes any purchases, draw up a contract and agree on what is allowed. (Examples: "Carpeting must stay." Or "Grandma's dresser may not be painted or altered in any way.") Spell out what the money must cover, like sales tax, shipping or delivery, assembly, or installation. Be specific about expectations, like signing off on a design before orders are placed.

The teen room makeover project can work at all budget levels. Perhaps that limits her to choosing new curtains and a rug. Or maybe the budget allows new hardwood floors and a whole new suite of furniture and bedding. Who knows? You're the parent: the parameters are in your hands. Just take advantage of the opportunity to teach about budgeting through a project your teen really wants to do.

TEACH ABOUT CONSEQUENCES

I've met parents who tightly control the décor of their kids' rooms, and the rooms either match the theme of the house or look straight off a page from the Pottery Barn Kids catalog. I encourage new parents to decorate the nursery in a way that appeals to them, but after the toddler years, it's time to loosen up a little. If you control every corner of your children's rooms, you may miss an opportunity to teach them how to make decisions and live with the consequences of their choices.

Even five-year-olds will likely have opinions about their room colors. Few will grasp the nuance of color, so their requests will probably be basic like "orange and green." They will be drawn to bright primary colors, so don't expect to get away with a soft sage green. No, if you want to honor your child's wishes, you are going to have to go with a juicy orange and a grassy green. There are a few ways you can work with what your young child wants, however, without driving yourself crazy.

First, you can paint three walls a neutral color like a soft, warm pewter or a creamy off-white and then ask your child to choose the accent wall color. Second, you can invite your child to choose *one* color for all four walls—just one. That helps your child develop an ability to prioritize and keeps the room from looking like a circus. Third, you can preselect three color options and ask which of the three he or she likes best. This gives a limited choice (a lot like real life). This approach works especially well for younger kids.

Involving your kids in the design of their rooms, like letting them choose their wall color, gives you a chance to make memories together.

By involving your kids in color choice, you get to spend time making memories together (especially if they are old enough to help with the painting, even if that just means helping spread out the drop cloths). You also help your children practice their decision-making and prioritizing skills. Perhaps best, they get to learn what it means to live with the consequences of their decisions. It's hard for kids to grasp the concept of a long-term choice, but try to talk about it anyway. When he's choosing his color, make sure he knows that accent wall will stay that color for a year, or three years, or until he gets his driver's license . . . some defined amount of time that makes sense for his age. No need to scare him away from a color he loves; just help him understand that neon green wall will be with him for quite a while. Then let him have it—there is no other way to learn. Who knows, maybe he really will love that color for the long haul! Remember, you can always close the door to his room.

TEACH ABOUT EMPOWERMENT

When I turned thirteen, I asked my parents for a bedroom makeover for my birthday. For as long as I could remember my room had been decorated in pink satin and frilly lace. I was ready for a grown-up room. Specifically I wanted a black-and-white room. They agreed to the change, and I ended up with a pretty great room, but there was one aspect of the experience that stayed with me and affects how I help my teen clients now. While my parents were awesome about making the changes, they also made a lot of the decisions for me, and I ended up with a black, white, *and gray* room instead of a black-and-white room. It's a small difference, but I had a pretty specific idea of what I wanted in my head, and it wasn't quite what I ended up with. I appreciated the effort my stepmom and dad put into the room, but at the same time I wished that they'd let me execute my full vision. (I think they might have feared that, given full rein, I would have ended up with a mostly black, goth, heavy metal kind of room.)

What I took away from that experience is a desire to empower my teen clients to express themselves as fully as possible in their rooms. The teen years are for stretching and growing and exploring personal boundaries. If a young adult is allowed to explore that within his own room, perhaps he won't feel as trapped and need to push harder and explore those boundaries as dramatically outside of the home.

I encourage you to let go of your "perfect" teen room vision, and let your preteen pick wild and random colors. Understand that a messy room isn't the end of the world, and you can always close the door when guests come. Yes, set boundaries—have nothing in the space that will be dangerous or lure bugs and rodents—but at the same time take a deep breath and know that it's just a room. With a door. That you can close.

Try not to rush the process: involve your kids in creating their space as much as you can. If you're hanging curtains, let your seven-year-old thread the curtains on the rod and tighten down the screws that anchor the rod to the brackets. If you're assembling Ikea furniture, let your ten-year-old identify and sort all of the components. If you're painting the walls, let your twelve-year-old roll on the paint. Sure, each task might take a little longer. The results might not be perfect. But what an opportunity to spend time with your kids and teach them valuable life lessons.

Your children will benefit from those special projects that teach them about big-picture concepts like budgeting, consequences, and empowerment. Meanwhile, day-to-day, you still have to manage all that stuff that comes with having kids in the house. So let's talk about three main spaces: the entry or mudroom, the family or living room, and your bedroom.

LAY OUT AN AWESOME LANDING ZONE

As you set up your home or choose a home for your growing family, pay special attention to the entry. Is there a space for shoes, coats, backpacks, and sports equipment? Without adequate space and planning for all this gear, you are guaranteeing years of frustration and arguments. It needn't be at the front door; it should be wherever the kids go in and out of the house every day. That might be through the garage or a side door.

If you are tight on space, think about both vertical and rotating storage. Vertical storage includes hooks on the walls and shelves built over doors and in corners. Rotating storage might involve bins that alternately hold winter and summer gear so that you only have the current season's stuff by the entry.

Work *with* the habits of your family as much as you can.

Work *with* the habits of your family as much as you can. If for years everyone has been wearing their shoes in the house, it's going to take time and effort (and perhaps tears) to change that habit. Consider replacing the entry and hall carpet with a wood, tile, or laminate that is easier to clean, and invest in a durable walk-off mat. If your kids are in the habit of dumping their backpacks and coats in a pile by the front door, forget about trying to convert them to using a cubby or locker. Install large kid-height hooks by the door instead: hooks are fast and easy to use, and it gets the coats and bags off the floor. Set up a system that's simple for kids to adapt to, and reward their efforts as they develop new habits, such as serving their favorite dessert at the end of a week of daily coat-hanging success.

FOCUS ON A FABULOUS FAMILY ROOM
In the family room, decide how much you need this to be a kid space or an adult space. In many family homes the kids pretty much take over every room. While it is great to let kids be kids and make them feel that this is their home as much as it is yours, there is something to be said for teaching kids boundaries. After all, when they are grown-ups they won't be allowed to spread work onto colleagues' desks and leave projects lying around the office. Help them know what is and is not their space, and how to pick up a project when they are done.

Again, work with the habits and ages of your kids. Use bins and baskets for collecting clutter; they work much better than the original packaging that kids' toys often come in. Some of that packaging is like a jigsaw puzzle that has to be solved just to put away the project. Who has the patience?

Over the years of working with families, I've identified three key tips for organizing kids' stuff:

1. Keep stuff low to the ground. People often forget to get down on the floor and see the world from a kid's perspective.
2. Keep it simple. Reduce steps for getting out and putting away items you want the kids to use. This applies especially to keeping a room clean. If an organizing system is too complicated, no one is going to use it—not even you.
3. Empower "doing it yourself." This not only raises capable kids, but also makes life easier on parents. For example, in the kitchen make sure it's just as easy for a kid to grab apple slices as chips. When you make things accessible, kids feel it was their idea in the first place.

There is no one-size-fits-all. Adapt the environment to your child's learning style. You'll increase the chances of success and reduce the opportunities for arguments.

PUT THE SEXY BACK IN YOUR BEDROOM

Until the 1970s most homes were dedicated to adult activities, and you'd have been hard-pressed to know that kids even lived there. That pendulum has swung completely to the other side, and nowadays kids' toys take over every nook and cranny of the house. Are kids running your household?

For both the good of the kids *and* the good of the parents, set limits and boundaries for at least a few spaces in your home. Yes, you are 100 percent a parent, but you are also an independent adult, a spouse, a daughter, a friend, a businessperson. If you can't see those other identities when you look around your home, you might lose sight of important parts of yourself, and your kids will miss a chance to understand what it means to grow up.

Clear boundaries in the home can teach your kids about growing up, turning them into much more pleasant and capable human beings.

The bedroom is a great place to create a space that is about you as an adult and a partner. Take a look at your master bedroom. If it is covered in laundry, kids' toys, junk mail, old magazines, or work, consider giving the room a makeover. If it holds a lot of memories of past relationships, do an emergency update. You need at least one space in the house that is a touchstone to you as a whole human: parent, partner, and independent person. Help the kids to understand that just like their room is for all *their* stuff (not their sibling's, or their friend's) your room is for all *your* stuff. Ask them to help you with this, perhaps using baskets to gather toys, mail, and laundry, and move it where it belongs.

If you create a grown-up retreat in your bedroom, you can wake up to a space that is soothing instead of stressful and go to sleep in a room that invites reading, romance, and rest. Your mind will be calmer, your body more rested, and your stamina raised to face the day's challenges waiting for you outside the bedroom door. Meanwhile, your kids will learn about respecting boundaries and the rights and requests of other people, turning them into much more pleasant and capable human beings.

Try some of the exercises below to start creating a kid-friendly *and* adult-friendly space.

Activity 27. Nooks and Crannies
Humans are instinctively drawn to cozy and safe nooks, and kids will create these spaces spontaneously with whatever is at hand. Take an afternoon to play fort or house with the kids. Gather up the pillows, blankets, boxes, and crates, and let the kids take charge. If you can, get your hands on some giant appliance boxes. Don't dictate the direction of play; just participate. You might find yourself defending your pirate castle from attack, cutting windows out of your box and making curtains for your new house, or selling fruit from your store. Imagination rules the kid universe!

Activity 28. Boundary Buddies
Teaching young kids about boundaries is important not only so you can carve out precious adult space in your home, but also because it will give them essential tools for dealing with their siblings, future college roommates, and even, one day, their spouses. In this activity, gather up the youngest members of your family and walk through the house like adventurers. Start by identifying the people a room might belong to. It might belong to one person (mine), to several people (theirs), or to the whole family (ours). In each space, ask the children who the room belongs to. Try not to give hints

at first: you might be surprised at their answers. As they successfully identify who each room belongs to, lightly discuss what that means. For example, after they identify their room as "mine," say "Yes! And that means you get to play in this room and keep your toys here, and they are safe. It also means you get to take care of this room." After they identify a room that is designed for the whole family, say "Yes! And that means we take care of it together and we share the space." And when they get to mommy or daddy's room, ask them who gets to keep their stuff in there, and who gets to take care of the space. You now have a shared language, which helps them understand, "This is mommy's room. Your toys don't sleep in this room; they get to sleep in your room."

Activity 29. Do-It-Themselves Design

Letting kids control their rooms can be scary, but it is also a safe way to let them stretch their wings and explore their personalities. At a young age, children are capable of choosing their paint color. Go with their desire for orange or pink or blue, but keep the majority of control by determining the intensity of the color and whether you cover all the walls or just one wall. Even at a young age, children can begin to understand choices and the consequences of their choices. When they pick the color, remind them to choose a color they really like because it will stay this color for at least a year (or however long you decide). If they grow tired of the color, help them understand it can change, but *not yet*.

Give older children more free rein. Done right, a kid's room makeover can teach the consequences of choice, budgeting, research, and of course, design skills. It can be a budget as low or high as you like, and you can require them to submit the plan and budget to you for final review. Try to be as hands-off as possible. Remember: you don't have to like it. The goal is *not* a perfectly designed room. It's that your kid gets to explore being a young adult in a safe way and learns essential adult survival tools.

Alternative Activity 30: Touch, Feel, and Tend Authentic Materials

In today's plastic world many kids don't touch glassware, metal silverware, or breakable dishes until age five, six, or even later. Although the impulse to equip kids with unbreakable objects is completely understandable, spilling and breaking can be important learning experiences. Find some heavy-duty glassware, safe metal silverware, and chunky china plates, and start letting your kids use them at dinnertime. Even if you do this once a week, Junior will begin to learn how to handle dishes with care. That can carry over into everything, from how he behaves at the dinner table, to how he treats his siblings and, later, partners and friends. We learn our habits early, and the home is the best place to learn responsibility and consideration. If you have trouble finding durable, authentic items, google "Montessori glassware." The Montessori schools use glass and metalware, and most have no plastic toys, so that can be a great resource. Or start with oversized shot glasses, which tend to be super strong!

TO SUM UP

Until the bittersweet day of empty-nesting comes along, aim to create a home that allows room for both playtime and quiet time, and accommodates both kid space and adult space.

Create organization systems that kids can help maintain. Set boundaries so you are not constantly fighting a rising tide of toys. And set aside places where the children can fully express themselves (such as their bedrooms) and other grown-up spaces where the children understand they are visitors and their toys leave with them (like your bedroom or office).

A home that allows both fun times within set boundaries and structure so that kids feel secure and know their limits (you know, so they can test them) can help you raise capable, confident, independent adults.

Chapter 9.
Happy and Single: Starting Again after Divorce or Widowhood

"Every new beginning comes from some other beginning's end."—Seneca

WHEN YOU LOSE THE ONE YOU LOVED, either through divorce or death, it rips your heart out no matter what the state of the relationship was before the loss. Even in a messy divorce it's not just the bad stuff that is ending, but also the dream you held when you walked down the aisle and said, "I do." In my work I have often found that both my widowed clients and my divorced clients are temporarily stuck in a quagmire of grief, uncertain about how to move forward.

What are the rules? When is it okay to let go of his clothes after he has passed away? Do you hold on to that expensive diamond ring after the divorce? Is it okay to remodel the master bath, or will that erase your memories of your wife soaking in that old bathtub? Are you remodeling the kitchen because you love to cook or out of spite because *he* never wanted to spend the money?

Losing, or leaving, a partner creates a lot of confusion, and it can be hard to trust your instincts, but your home can help you heal and emerge stronger. As you open yourself, and your home, to love again, look to Chapter 5 for more guidance.

There are two diametrically opposed questions to consider when thinking about what to do with traces of your lost lover in your home:

- **How do you honor the past?**
- **How do you let go of the past?**

Whether you've experienced a divorce or faced the death of a loved one, there may be many reasons why you want to honor your history as much as you want to let go of the past. If your partner has died, you may have no wish to erase them from your life. Even after a divorce, you might want to honor that history because, whether the memories of your marriage are good or bad, that relationship shaped who you are today. For example, while that print you bought in Australia might evoke sad memories of an ended marriage, it also might remind you of the first time you conquered your fear of heights and bungee jumped. Additionally, honoring the past might come up because, even if you're tempted to destroy every last reminder of your ex, you have a responsibility to manage the relationship on behalf of your kids. As an example, one of my most treasured possessions is a birthday card my parents gave me before they divorced, signed "Mom and Dad."

After divorce or the death of a partner, how you honor the past in your home will depend on whether at first you want to change everything—or nothing.

HEALING AFTER WIDOWHOOD: CHANGING EVERYTHING

Let's acknowledge that, when your partner has passed away, there are *no* rules to driving this road, and you will have to trust your intuition to steer you to the answers. If you sometimes get it "wrong" (i.e., if you regret decisions later), be gentle with yourself and know that you are only human. It's okay to be less than perfect.

My widowed client, Cynthia, who was in her seventies, chose to remodel her entire condo when her partner passed away. Some people in her life considered this frivolous, or accused her of wanting to erase all memories of him, or shamed her for spending so much money too late in her life. Cynthia and I worked together closely for months, and I can promise you that nothing in her actions dishonored her partner or overstretched her budget. The condo was looking tired and outdated, and she planned to spend the rest of her life there; she also knew her partner would have wanted her to be happy. Although we shed some tears as we designed the space that would be her forever home, most of the memories she shared with me were joyful. What's more, by having a designer and a contractor in her life during the year after his death, Cynthia had regular visits from friendly people as she passed through all the firsts that come after someone dies: the first birthday, the first Valentine's Day, the first Thanksgiving.

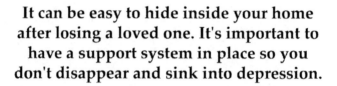

It can be easy to hide inside your home after losing a loved one. It's important to have a support system in place so you don't disappear and sink into depression.

Your home is an easy space to hide in after your loss. It's important to have a support system in place so you don't disappear and sink into depression. If you were a naturally social person before your loss or divorce, you might consider making some changes to your public spaces if you are up to it so that you have an "excuse" to invite people over. If in the past your home has been an obstacle to having people over, do what it takes to eliminate that obstacle. A word of warning: If you hire help to update your space, be *extremely careful*. Unscrupulous people have been known to take advantage of people who are in pain. Have a friend by your side as you get involved with any large-scale projects and do only what feels right to you now. You can always take on more later.

HEALING AFTER WIDOWHOOD: CHANGING NOTHING

Some who are working through grief and loss go to the opposite extreme: they keep everything *exactly* the way it was. This is okay, but it should not go on forever. A century and a half ago, when Prince Albert died suddenly, Queen Victoria plummeted into lifelong mourning, inconsolable into old age. It wasn't that she *couldn't* move on but that *she chose not to*. She divided her time between a palace next to his tomb and their Highlands love nest, surrounded by locks of his hair and other mementos. No one can move on when stuck so firmly in the past. To me that seems a sad way to spend decades of your life. Your partner would be glad to know you loved them, but would be heartbroken to see you throw your life and vitality away. They would wish for you joy and new adventures, not a stagnant life as if you too had passed away. Grieve, but in time, discover the beauty of unexplored places and let new love into your life, even if that just means a new hobby or pet.

Part of honoring your partner after their death is to live a new, vital life of your own while still holding their memory in your heart.

I won't pretend to know how long is long enough to grieve your loss, but I can say that your home can be a great place to test the waters before moving on. Whether it's been a month or a year, you can try small steps (repainting the guest room or reorganizing the spice rack) to see how it feels. Start in rooms not directly connected with your spouse, like the guest room rather than his office. This way you can try on change without feeling like you've just wiped away the memory of your partner. Little by little, you can let go of the things he or she used every day, until all you are left with are the handful of precious reminders you need to keep close to your heart to honor their memory.

A final note: It's best not to get involved in a new relationship if you can't quite bring yourself to remove your former spouse's possessions from your home. That can be unfair to your new partner. When you are ready to love again, you'll be ready to make room for that new special loved one.

HEALING AFTER DIVORCE: WHEN TO LET GO

> "If you want to forget something or someone, never hate it, or never hate him/her. Everything and everyone that you hate is engraved upon your heart; if you want to let go of something, if you want to forget, you cannot hate."
> —C. JoyBell C.

Post-divorce, you might have trouble letting go of things from your past marriage because they are *your* memories too. Mostly it requires honesty.

When you look at that souvenir from your trip with your ex, do you feel more than 50 percent happy, or more than 50 percent sad? Rarely is that emotion split right down the middle. If you are more happy than sad, keep it—it's part of your past and the path that made you the wonderful person you are today. If you are more sad than happy, it's time to create a new memory.

If you really can't decide if an item makes you more happy than sad, put it in a box (or toss a sheet over it if it's huge) and store it in the garage. Mark a date on the calendar three months away, then revisit the item. If you didn't miss it while it was stored away, or if you are overwhelmed with sadness when you unwrap it, for goodness sake, get rid of it. Either way the item isn't doing you any good.

It. Is. Just. Stuff.

Be honest with yourself when it's time to face whether you are keeping an item in response to a negative emotion such as spite or guilt. These emotions taste good the way ice cream tastes good: short-term satisfaction with no long-term benefit. Wallowing in those emotions by holding on to the old stuff in your home won't help you build a fulfilling life. The objects will remain obstacles to your highest success. Spite shows up when you keep an item not because you care about it but because you know your spouse loved it and there is *no* way you are giving it back. Guilt shows up when you know that you don't actually want a thing in your life, but it "cost" too much (either in actual money or in divorce negotiations) to part with.

Let. It. Go.

If you're not Zen enough to give it back to your ex, donate it so someone else can use it. Don't let stuff hold you back from living your best life now.

YEARS LATER: WHEN STUFF BUBBLES UP

> **"I don't see divorce as a failure. I see**
> **it as the end to a story. In a story,**
> **everything has an end and a beginning."**
> **—Olga Kurylenko**

All this letting go may or may not happen right after your divorce. At some point you'll have to deal with it, even if it's just because you are moving from one house to another and have to pack it all up.

Even years after a divorce, it can be a struggle to let go of the stuff from a past relationship. Sometimes the letting-go process opens up old wounds. Sometimes all that stuff overwhelms you and you don't know where to begin. Oftentimes it's both too much stuff and too many emotions. Even if you're better off without your ex, you mourn your "failure" at something so socially and culturally momentous as marriage.

Again, there are no rules. A lovely client of mine was four years past her relationship before she could deal with the stuff her ex-husband had left behind—forgotten yearbooks, decades-old tax records, and his old CD collection. Even though it was abundantly clear her ex had no intention of collecting his belongings, and none of it had any personal meaning to her, it took her four years to gather enough courage to remove it.

Don't judge yourself too harshly if you aren't moving on at the rate your friends or family think you should. Sometimes it is better to let things settle and see how you feel in a month or two before you burn it all to the ground. Some choices are irreversible, so it's wise to let things percolate a bit before you take drastic action, like destroying his vintage car. Sitting with your pain, grief, or confusion for a bit can be okay. Then you can test out small changes in your home to see how it feels to move forward. Sleep on the other side of the bed. Get rid of the big screen TV. Replace the white dinner dishes with something bright and cheery. Add whimsical throw pillows to the sofa. Bring in small touches that say "you"—anything that helps you look toward your future instead of your past. It may feel uncomfortable at first because it is unfamiliar. But just because it's unfamiliar doesn't make it bad. After all, hope always comes wrapped in the packaging of the unknown.

Leaving things the way they were when your ex lived in the house can be a lot like stubbing your toe day after day on the footboard of your bed. If it hurts like crazy every day, why not get a new bed? Little shifts will go a long way toward moving you out of the divorce and into your next chapter. Clean out your cupboards and put your dishes in a new spot. Move the silverware to a different drawer. As my colleague and fellow divorcée Mariah Beckman says, "No one explains how hard it can be just to put the dishes away in the same cupboard, or sit on the couch where you used to unwind as a couple, once you divide your life with a separation."

After my divorce I spent several months looking at what I had accumulated and picked out with my ex: the sofa, the print over the fireplace, the wall colors. One day I'd just had enough. Overnight, I couldn't stand looking backward anymore, wondering why it had all fallen apart. Why I had *failed*. It wasn't going to change, so I figured I might as well move on. That's when I started painting the walls and selling my stuff on Craigslist and sleeping in my little twin bed built for one. I knew they were not forever choices, but they didn't have to be. I just needed to cross the finish line of my old life. It was utterly and completely transformative. That finish line turned into a starting line, and I felt refreshed and ready to run to the beat of my own heart.

OUT WITH THE OLD

Take the time you need to heal, create a cocoon in which you can take shelter for a while, then emerge as a beautiful new butterfly. If you're long past that breakup and whining about how all you want is to be in a loving relationship again, take an honest look around your home and read Chapter 5, Happy and in Love: Embracing Romance and Companionship. Does your house look like the home of someone ready for love? Or are you that person who keeps saying you want to find new love but your home looks exactly like it did when your ex lived there? If you want "in with the new," don't forget the "out with the old" part of the equation.

DIVORCE AND THE HOME: WHEN YOU HAVE KIDS

> **"All the art of living lies in a fine mingling**
> **of letting go and holding on."**
> **—Havelock Ellis**

Of course, if you have kids, you know the ghosts of your marriage will linger long after your divorce, whether you like it or not. You might be more than ready to eliminate every last trace of your ex, but for your kids' sake, it's your job to hold onto things that are important. Later on your children may have questions and will need touchstones to understand that a divorce doesn't take away the love parents have for their kids, even when they are bad at showing that love and may be behaving like children themselves. Yep, it's yet another one of those moments, fair or not, that you get to practice being a grown-up because you're the parent.

You don't have to figure out what may or may not be worth keeping. It's okay to box things up a little at a time and put them in some dark corner of the garage labeled with your kids' names. They might never ask about the stuff, or they might ask ten years down the road, or they might throw a tantrum the very next week. No matter what, you'll be ready, because while you may have taken the mementos out of sight, you didn't toss them. Good for you!

Does that mean you have to keep everything associated with your ex? No way! And there is one room in the house you should definitely reinvent: your bedroom. Get new sheets. Move the bed to another wall. Scrub it top to bottom. Vacuum your dresser drawers and toss out anything that's stained or ripped. Add beautiful lamps to the side tables, and have the carpets steam cleaned. Add a fresh coat of paint and, while you're at it, ask your kids if they want to repaint their rooms. They might enjoy it, or they might want their spaces to stay intact for a while—either way is okay. They may have questions about why you are changing Mommy or Daddy's room, and it's a teachable moment for them to understand that your ex has his or her own bedroom now, and you both get to choose new paint colors for your own bedrooms. You're all in this together, and learning to let go is also a part of growing up.

No matter what, change the bedding.

DIVORCE AND THE HOME: RESIST THE IMPULSE TO COMPETE WITH YOUR EX

"Don't fight a battle if you don't gain anything by winning." —Erwin Rommel

When it comes to putting down roots for you and the kids after a divorce, guard against the desire to keep up with or compete with your ex. It's a losing battle. Don't engage. You will never, ever gain your children's affection or loyalty through gifts and material things (though you will find that the kids catch on to the game in a heartbeat and play it for all that it is worth). You can, however, deeply impact how the divorce will affect the kids through the choices you make about your post-divorce home. It *is* important to create a home that feels safe and inviting. (Again, that doesn't imply expensive.)

A colleague once revealed what I think is a common scenario. After her parents divorced, she said she dreaded going to her dad's place. It was unkempt and dark, and lacked any comfortable furniture. She realized that, although she loved her dad, his dreary home affected how often she wanted to see him. You may not be a natural at setting up a home, but there are many professionals out there who can help. Ask for assistance, but also use caution. Just like with widowers, divorced, vulnerable people are targets for unscrupulous folks. Insist on a contract and be sure you understand it. If you are feeling uncomfortable, put on the brakes. Trust your intuition.

Activity 31: Ghost Hunting

Let's hunt down any ghosts that may be haunting your home. Go room by room, and list any object that reminds you of a past relationship. Read through the list and explore how you feel. Circle the items that make you feel especially icky, and make a plan for eliminating those objects.

Three items that need to leave my home:

_____   by date: _____
_____   by date: _____
_____   by date: _____

Activity 32. Attracting New Energy into the Bedroom

If you are moving on from a past relationship, start by fully clearing your bedroom and banishing the old energy.

1. Flip your mattress.
2. Sleep on the other side of the bed or right down the middle.
3. Move your bedroom to another room.
4. Buy new sheets and pillowcases. Consider a new mattress.
5. Open the windows and clean them inside and out.
6. If you haven't already done so, get rid of any toys (plush or otherwise) or undergarments that your ex brought into your relationship.
7. Repaint the walls and, ideally, the ceiling.
8. Clean it top to bottom, even under the bed.
9. Add more light by changing your bulbs or bringing in a new lamp.
10. Bring in something new—not because your ex would hate it but because you love it.

Three changes I will make to my bedroom:

_____   by date: _____
_____   by date: _____
_____   by date: _____

TO SUM UP

Love can't guarantee a happy ending, and many of us will face the loss of a partner either through divorce or death. If you find yourself surrounded by memories of that former partner, you can reinvent yourself, and your home, so you emerge stronger and more resilient, ready to turn the end of that story into the beginning of a new one. It's up to you: Do you want to live in a place that haunts you with painful memories, or one that gives you refuge from life's storms? Make sure your home is doing its job and launching you forward, not holding you back.

Chapter 10.
Happy and Empty-Nested: Discovering Opportunities

"Childhood is a short season."
—Helen Hayes

LOVE SOMETIMES MEANS LETTING GO, but it's not always because of a breakup. One of the most bittersweet moments in a parent's life is when it's time to let the kids fly from the nest (or, as in my own case, push them out of the nest). If you are in a partnership or marriage, whether you like it or not, your relationship is about to undergo a major shift—it's like part of your marriage leaves along with the kids. At this moment, your home plays an important new role in your life.

THE LAST TWO STANDING

First, if you're married when the kids leave the nest, the relationship of the last two people standing in the house may need some redefining. How are you going to spend your time together? Do you have activities in common that don't involve kids? Is the house too big for just the two of you? Maybe you see yourself using all that room to host the family as it grows with grandkids. Perhaps it's time to makeover the kids' rooms or remodel the kitchen and create a place perfect for entertaining.

You and your partner may have different expectations about what will happen next. He may be thinking of a trip to Europe; you might have your heart set on a new kitchen. Just because you shared the same dream a decade ago doesn't mean you're on the same page now. Tread lightly: a simple statement about what you are going to do to Junior's room could set off an avalanche of emotion you did not expect. If you're not sure what is on your partner's mind, ask. If it feels like a touchy subject, try reframing it: talk about a friend who remodeled or an inspiring magazine article about a couple who traveled to Peru. Then bite your tongue and let him talk without interruption. Once you know what is on his mind you can begin a loving conversation.

FLYING SOLO ONCE THE KIDS LEAVE THE NEST
On the other hand, if you are single when the kids move out, you are in a position to do just about any darn thing you want. A bit like getting divorced, you suddenly have very little in the way of commitments and little to lose. It's an opportunity to do something a little crazy, a little scary, or both. Like one of my clients chose to do, you could finally take those ballroom dance lessons, put up a wall of mirrors, and turn your living room into a practice studio. Or, now that not every penny needs to go toward the kids, you can make over your living room and start inviting your friends over for game nights. It's a moment to figure out who the "new you" will be.

Empty-nesting creates an opportunity to do things that feel a little crazy and a little scary. It's a chance to discover and define a "new you."

Now that you're single and child-free, bringing a romantic partner home might be less complicated, more carefree. It might mean a new level of sensual freedom. (Um, you might ask your kids for their keys back if you're going to be wandering around naked.) Do you welcome romance into your now-empty nest? Are your kitchen and living room date ready? How about your bedroom? Or are you perfectly happy being single? That's okay too!

PARENTING YOUR KIDS ON THEIR WAY OUT THE DOOR
Whether you are single or partnered, be intentional as you ease the kids into their adult lives. Sure, hold on to your kids' stuff for a few years until they get settled into their own places, but be careful that your home doesn't become

either a museum or a junkyard for all their stuff. A garage full of childhood toys, furniture you thought they'd want, and sports equipment they haven't used in years—all these things send a message that they needn't take responsibility for their stuff. A house frozen in time, as if the kids might come back and be children again, sends a message that you are stagnant, and now that your life as a kids-at-home parent is over, there is nothing left to do but cling to the past. Yes, it's bittersweet, but to stay vibrant and vital, make sure your home changes with you. It's not only good for you, it's good for your kids too.

SORTING THROUGH THE STUFF: JUST DO IT

If you are like most people, you've spent decades collecting stuff, and very little time letting stuff go. You may have piles of artwork and paperwork from your kids' school years. You may have closets full of memorabilia from your own childhood and young adult years. You may even have boxes of stuff from your parents' home.

Go through it all and eliminate what you can. Why now? First, it might be a burden on you. You probably don't know what's buried in those boxes, and even if there were something important, you'd never find it. That creates unconscious stress that you carry with you at all times, and unconscious stress diminishes your joy and suppresses your immune system. Second, if you choose to ignore it all, you will be creating a burden for someone else. When you do ultimately pass on from this life, someone, perhaps your child, will be standing in the middle of your home, not only overcome by grief but also overwhelmed by all the stuff. If you think *you* are overwhelmed by the piles, imagine how someone else will cope.

Activity 33. Memories: Sorting Through Childhood Stuff

It will never be easier than it is today. Here are some strategies for facing those piles:

1. Start small. If you have a four-drawer filing cabinet full of paper, just pull out a one- or two-inch pile and sort it. If you have a garage filled to the rafters with stuff, just address a tiny portion—a two-foot by two-foot area, or one box, or just one big piece of exercise equipment that is blocking the rest. The key is to make progress, so every bite you take, whether one a day or one a week, should give you a feeling of accomplishment.

2. Make it a habit. Sorting in small bites works best if you keep at it. Make a fifteen- to thirty-minute daily practice of sorting, and give yourself permission to stop after those fifteen to thirty minutes. It will seem like small progress, but like drops of water in a bucket you'll find the bucket full, or your garage empty, before you know it!

3. Challenge yourself with bottom-line questions: When was the last time I looked for or thought of this? Would someone else enjoy this item and memory, and could I share it with them instead? If I didn't have this, would I really miss it? Here are two techniques I use on myself:

   - **If there were a fire . . .** When I am sorting for myself and I feel stuck, I ask myself these questions: "If my house were to burn down, is this an object that I would miss? Would it make me feel heartsick to lose it?" More often than not the answer is no.

   - **Is this memory already represented?** Oftentimes we have boxes full of stuff that all represent the same memory when in reality we only need one item to bring back the joy, flavors, scents, and full experience of a memory. For example, your dear aunt may have given you her twelve place settings of fine china. Do you need all of those settings to carry that memory, or perhaps just a few select pieces, and the rest could go to other family members? Do you need every drawing your children ever created, or would one from each grade evoke all the memories of their school years? See if you can edit down to one item to represent each memory or chapter of your life.

With all that in mind, choose a pile in your house today that needs downsizing and go spend fifteen minutes letting go of at least one or two items. That's it. Just that small step is a giant leap to a freer, lighter, more agile life for you and those who come after you.

Go do it now, then come back and record your success.

Today, I let go of:

_____

_____

_____

_____

and I feel:

_____

_____

_____

_____

Activity 34. Something I've Always Wanted to Do

Take a few minutes to brainstorm all the things you've wished you could try. Try not to filter as you make the list: dream big, as if all things are possible. Whether you are forty, sixty, or beyond, you have decades ahead to develop a new skill or take on a new challenge. For ideas, google "bucket list ideas." For more inspiration, read *Never Too Late: My Musical Life Story* by John Holt or *The Late Starters Orchestra* by Ari L. Goldman.

Now circle one wish that would be easy to try, and make a plan for starting that new activity within one month. Then circle one wish that feels like a stretch. Next to that activity, write down three small steps you can take or resources you can look into to make it a reality. Then make a plan for executing, researching, or getting hold of that resource within the next month.

By developing new passions, you will not only make the most of this third chapter in your life but also inspire your kids to know that there is life after empty-nesting. You'll continue the work of being a good parent by setting a marvelous, vibrant example.

Example List:

Live for a month in Italy	Visit my family's homeland
Learn to make sushi	Try a new hairstyle or color
Learn to knit	Go on a meditation retreat
Volunteer for Habitat for Humanity	Finish that craft project
Join a book club	Learn Portuguese

My wish list—what I've always wanted to do:

_____   _____

_____   _____

_____   _____

_____   _____

_____   _____

TO SUM UP

Love inevitably means letting go, especially when it comes to your children. You'll always be their parent, but now your kids get to go live their own lives and that means a new chapter for you too. Show them there is life after empty-nesting, and reshape your home to support new interests and hobbies. Whether you update the space and prepare to host big family gatherings, or you downsize to a new space that suits your new chapter, renew your home in a way that makes you feel alive and helps you look forward, not back.

Chapter 11.
Happy and Creative:
Living Playfully at Any Age

> "The supreme accomplishment is to
> blur the line between work and play."
> —Arnold J. Toynbee

NOTHING MAKES YOU FEEL AS ALIVE as being playful or creative. In play we can bend the rules, try new ways of seeing the world, test out ideas and boundaries, and just let go of all the expectations. Creative play is how we learn and adapt. It is essential for our survival.

At the same time, play can be serious business. Play teaches us important lessons as children and keeps us young as adults. If you've ever watched a litter of puppies you've seen them wrestle and tumble, playfully attacking each other with abandon and joy. Each nip of the teeth lets the puppies explore what it means to be family and learn about hierarchies and limits. We play to understand what it means to be family, how to get along in society, and how to push boundaries, and it all starts in the nest. Have you created safe space in your home for play and discovery, or is everything serious, a place where you must be careful and the rules are strictly laid out?

Play helps us understand
what it means to be part of a family
and how to get along in society at large.

Play encourages us to learn how to interact with others socially. Play teaches children how to communicate verbally and nonverbally, negotiate, take turns, take charge, and experiment with different roles in a group or in society. Play is unparalleled in learning how to work through differences and conflicts around space, materials, and rules, without long-term consequences that would otherwise come by learning those lessons "the hard way."

IT'S NOT JUST KID STUFF

Play is just as important for adults as it is for children. Our history of play as children and the practice of play as adults make it possible to handle grown-up life. From a round of golf or game of poker to office politics and marriage, we constantly draw on the skills we learned at recess as we negotiate feelings of success, competition, and failure, and try to deal fairly and lightheartedly with others in our daily lives. And as much as we like to groan about them, team-building exercises, done right, are adult versions of play that can, in fact, create work environments where the group is better equipped to communicate, collaborate, and understand differing points of view.

Play encourages not only collaboration but also creative expression. Artist Judith Shaw writes that "creativity is an exploration of our inner selves . . . Creative expression keeps us in touch with our intuition. The better our intuition is, the easier it is to make correct decisions and move with the flow of life." Any artist, writer, or other creative person can tell you that to explore your art, you must let go of perfect and embrace *what is*. It takes courage to be bad at something—sometimes really, really bad—in order to uncover something beautiful. That, in turn, prepares us for real life with all its challenges, failures, and tests of our faith. Shaw adds, "Regular creative practice requires a certain kind of courage which can spill over into your daily life allowing you to move from fear to fearlessness."

If we can agree that play and creativity are essential ingredients to full and meaningful lives, how do you set up a home that invites playfulness and creativity? First, make sure that there are spaces that welcome play and creativity—it's hard to explore ideas when you feel constricted by too many rules. Second, create a secure and safe environment, since neither play nor creativity can be realized when you're bound by uncertainty or fear. Third, recognize that your tastes and preferences in play and creative activities will change as you age, so stay flexible. Change is natural: embrace it.

PLAY IN ORDER TO LIVE

**"Men do not quit playing because
they grow old; they grow old
because they quit playing."
—Oliver Wendell Holmes Jr.**

How we set up our homes has everything to do with how we foster play and creativity in ourselves and in our families, but there is no one set way to accomplish this. One of my clients has a joy-filled home adorned with her kids' bright drawings all over the walls. We're not talking about drawings on paper, mind you. The kids literally draw on the yellow walls in the living room, dining room, and hallway. That might drive you crazy, but this family loves it. You certainly can't argue with the creativity that this home encourages!

Another client has a tightly curated gallery wall of art done by family members—all framed and strikingly displayed on a slate-blue accent wall in a way that honors both their creativity and their need for calm and order.

A third client has set up trapeze equipment in her living room. Another ditched nearly all her furniture so she could host partner-yoga parties. And yet another installed a wall of mirrors so she could practice her ballroom dancing at home.

There are no rules to what it means to be creative at home, but it is important to set aside play space that's right for you and your family. Maybe your family loves to play outdoors. You'll need a good landing zone for when all the outdoor enthusiasts come home, and accessible storage for all the fishing, camping, or sports gear. Without a space to store and access the equipment, you'll either come to hate the sport as you trip over soccer equipment, or you'll find that your favorite activity fades away when it just becomes too much trouble to dig out the skis. On the other hand, when all your gear is easy to find and ready to go when you are, you'll spend a lot less time hunting it down or tripping over it and a lot more time outdoors, where you love to be.

Whether your playtime means having friends over for a whisky-and-poker night, taking the dog out for rounds of fetch, or writing the novel that has been inside of you for decades, you'll be glad you invested the time to set up a home that supports your fun and creativity. Why not create a space that makes it easy to have your friends over for game night, to find the leash and tennis ball, or to let the novel come to life?

MAKE PLAYING AS EASY AS PIE

If you want to play more—do puzzles, practice the guitar, rebuild classic cars—you must have a space that makes it easy to settle into the activity without too much hassle. Place the puzzles out on a game table. Hang the guitar on the wall in your den. Declutter the garage so you have a place to tinker. The more you can leave the tools of the hobby out and ready to use, the more likely it is that you'll dive back in again. You'll need an easy bridge from a serious day at work to a creative evening of play, so think about preparing some environmental cues. If you're a writer, prepare a desk space that *looks* like a writer's space. If you are an artist, leave your easel out, your paints laid out ready to use. Set up environmental cues that help shake off whatever else is on your mind and get you into a creative state, ready for art and play.

The more you can leave the tools of your hobby out and ready to use, the more likely it is that you'll dive in and practice your art.

Play and creativity are habits, and like any habit it can take a while for it to come naturally. Writing that first chapter, taking those first hesitant waltz steps, pushing yourself out the door for that soccer game when it's cold and rainy—these habits need the right gear and the right environment, especially during the fragile time when you are just starting the new hobby. A space that encourages you to try something new, rather than a space that defeats you before you even begin, makes your journey possible.

"The ache for home lives in all of us, the safe place where we can go as we are and not be questioned." —Maya Angelou

R e b e c c a   W e s t

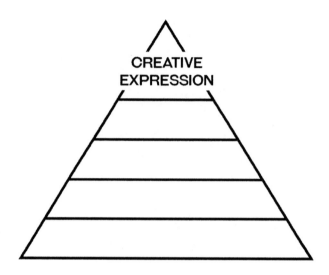

The second key to nurturing creativity is to provide a safe and secure home. Who can enjoy play when they feel uneasy, scrutinized, or judged? Creativity lies at the very top of the pyramid of Maslow's hierarchy of needs in the category of self-actualization. Ideally, your home should foster security, love, and acceptance. In a secure environment, you can realize your most creative self. Unfortunately, the places many people call home fail to meet the needs of those who live there, and that keeps the occupants from reaching their creative potential or willingly venturing out to explore the world in play.

**When we feel safe we feel
freer to explore and can realize
our most creative potential.**

In *The Power of Place*, author Winifred Gallagher mentions the work of psychologist Stephen Suomi, who studies primate behavior. In one of Suomi's research studies, he let the primates out of their quarters to run free in a play area. Each one ventured out to play and explore, the boldest going first and the timid following, but as Suomi observed, "However adventurous, they all charge back to their home cage several times in the course of an hour, as if making sure it was still there." It's much the same for humans: having that secure home base makes it possible for us to go and explore and play. As Suomi summarized, "A secure base is a safe haven to explore from and return to when the world feels dicey."

As a kid I felt secure because my parents created a safe haven at every military base we moved to. I knew my home would be there waiting for me as I ventured out to make new friends. It is so much easier to explore when you know that the world is stable under your feet.

EMBRACE CHANGE: IT'S HEALTHY!

> **"Change isn't made by asking permission. Change is made by asking forgiveness, later." —Seth Godin**

A third way to encourage play and creativity is to make way for new hobbies over time and give everyone permission to change interests. Your kids are probably not going to play with Legos and Barbies forever, right? Likewise, you may lose interest in knitting or woodworking, and your partner might decide he's done with golf and would rather host a monthly wine club instead.

Shifts in hobbies and interests can be challenging for parents and kids alike. I know I found it really hard to accept when my mom's interest in sewing faded out. My whole childhood had been defined by her sitting at the sewing machine for hours, sewing clothes and household items, crafting with me in the sewing room. I'd organize the bobbins; she'd teach her classes. When she moved on to jewelry making and metalsmithing, and then later to oil painting, it was kind of tough to get my head around the idea that my mom wasn't a seamstress. I felt sure she would miss it and go back to sewing some day. It took me many years to get that this just wasn't her anymore. Of course she was still a vibrant, creative woman, but she was channeling her creativity in a new form.

Even when you don't understand why your spouse or child has shed an interest, be assured that exploring, growing, and changing is part of the human experience and must be allowed, even encouraged. That doesn't mean it won't be frustrating at times. Perhaps it was easier to give your sister gifts when she was really into her scrapbooking hobby, but now she's abandoned it. Or you just spent a fortune on cheerleading camp, and now your daughter wants to join the field hockey team instead. Regardless, there are times to move on from our creative outlets, and if we love our family and ourselves, we will let that evolution happen. There is so much to be tried and explored in this world! My husband and I rarely do the same thing twice, not because it wasn't the most fun, awesome experience ever, but because there are just too many neat places to go, foods to try, and people to meet. We'd love to go back, but we just don't have the time.

You can adapt nearly any activity to any age, and certainly to any gender.

As you set up your creative home, try not to make assumptions about what can or cannot be done at a certain age. Aside from safety considerations (like not letting a six-year-old play with fire unsupervised), you can adapt nearly any activity to any age, and certainly to any gender. Try not to dissuade your daughter from "dirty" or "dangerous" hobbies. If you wouldn't hesitate to let your son try it, let your daughter try it too. And avoid putting limits on yourself or your parents as you age. My mother took on hang gliding at age fifty. Yes, it took her a little longer to heal from bumps and bruises than it would have at age thirty, but she had a blast. If you need a little inspiration, check out the two books I suggested in Chapter 10: Ari L. Goldman's *The Late Starters Orchestra* or John Holt's *Never Too Late: My Musical Life Story*. Remember, if you pick up a violin for the first time at age fifty, you could be concert grade at age seventy. No matter what, you'll be better than if you'd never picked it up at all.

With the following exercises, you'll explore changes that encourage a more creative and playful home.

Activity 35. The Curse of the Incomplete Craft Project
In this exercise, you'll take an honest assessment of all the half-done projects in the house, including those for which you have all the supplies but have yet

to begin the work. List any unfinished creative project, which might include quilting, craft kits, model kits, knitting projects, jewelry making or beading projects, computer rebuilding, clock tinkering, canning, candy making, flower pressing, vintage car rebuilding, mosaics, retiling the floor, painting a room, sewing curtains, and so on. By each, list the person who started the project, when it was started (if ever), the last time someone worked on it, and when the supplies were purchased (add more pages if needed):

Project:	Artist:	Date begun:

When the list is complete, talk with the family about this crafty to-do list. Which projects are no longer of interest? Which ones were forgotten? Which ones can you complete as a family? Which ones can you take off the to-do list by taking the whole kit and caboodle to Goodwill, school, or a community center? Remember, it's okay to say that you're no longer interested in it. There is no failure inherent in moving on to something new, even if the supplies were expensive. Life is too short to spend it working on something meaningless, and someone else might be overjoyed to receive the supplies. Perhaps it was a waste of money, but are you going to make it a waste of your time too? Money is just money, but there is nothing more precious than time.

Activity 36. Crafty Commitments

After you've finished Activity 35 (an honest assessment of all the half-done projects in the house) and eliminated the craft projects you've lost interest in, it's time to consider why the other projects are not getting done. So, start a new list of the projects each person wants to finish. As a family, commit to changes that will help each person have creative time to finish his or her projects. Maybe you'll clear out space in the garage for model building. Maybe you'll rearrange the hall closet so supplies are readily at hand. Maybe you'll establish a weekly or monthly family craft night. Together, brainstorm

ways to carve out creative space and time for each family member in a way
that suits each person:

Project:	Artist:	Possible solutions:

Activity 37. Promised Playtime

Play comes in many forms, from having imaginary friends, to playing board
games and video games, to participating in sports, to just having a beer and
telling jokes or spooky stories around a backyard fire pit. My husband and
I regularly play word games to pass the time while standing in line. Play is
for all ages. It keeps minds sharp and faces smiling.

Nothing is worse, though, than forced play. How many times did I skip
gym class so I could get out of playing dodge ball? Ugh. So as you are thinking about ways to foster play in your home, be sure to include your family
in the brainstorming process. You might be surprised by the results. I was
surprised when I chatted with my staff about employee retreats. Personally,
I would have jumped at the chance to do a ropes course, a classic team-building exercise, but it turns out that my lead team member would rather walk
barefoot on glass than face a ropes course. Not the best team-building activity for my group after all.

(By the way, if you're a parent and your kids want to try a zip line, I say
suck it up and do it. Better for the person in power to bend a little. But use
your judgment: if you are truly acrophobic, trying to face that fear might not
result in a great family outing if you literally freeze up and delay everyone
else waiting for their turn.)

For this exercise, gather up the family and brainstorm ways to play
together more often. First, make a giant list of all the things you could do
together. Remember, this is brainstorming, so no editing allowed: there are
no bad ideas at this stage. If your four-year-old suggests you all get in a
rocket and fly to the moon, write it down!

Next, write down the resources each activity will take, including supplies, time, travel, money, and people. In the last column, note the major obstacle to the idea. Now identify two easy activities that you could actually do this week and one more activity that would be a bit of a stretch to accomplish. Pick one of the two easy activities and put it on the calendar for sometime in the next ten days. (The younger your kids are, the sooner you need to make it happen, since even one day is a Very Long Time for a little kid.) Consider making a countdown calendar or paper chain for the days leading to Playtime. Then pick the stretch activity and start planning. Try to choose activities that everyone is on board with. If you can't get everyone to agree, that's okay: choose two easy and two stretch activities.

The *most* important part of this exercise is the execution. Planning to play is not the same as playing.

Example ideas for kids and for adults (I can honestly say I have done all but two of these as an adult):

- Throw a half-birthday or half-holiday party (a party thrown exactly six months before the actual event).
- Take dance lessons.
- Host a game night.
- Bake cookies.
- Ride bikes to the park.
- Have a transportation day: try to use as many different forms of transportation in one day as possible.
- Take a mini road trip allowing only left turns.
- Get dressed up in fancy clothes for no reason and have dinner at a fast food restaurant. Extra points for '80s prom dresses.
- Play hide-and-seek.
- Go on a scavenger hunt.
- Dance through family chore time.
- Draw on the sidewalk with chalk.
- Play miniature golf. Extra points if in costumes.
- Watch a TV competition show (like a singing or cooking contest) and vote for who you think the judges will pick by pausing before voting takes place and getting everyone's guesses. Have a prize for the winner if you want.

Ways we could have more playtime as a family:

Things we could do:	Time it would take:	What we need to change to do this:
_____	_____	_____
_____	_____	_____
_____	_____	_____
_____	_____	_____

Activity 38. New Adventures, Old Loves

This activity gives you a chance to reflect on the ways you have changed, to let go of habits that are no longer serving you, and even return to an old project if you are so moved. Use the blank spaces to write down how you used to play, how you play now or feel you ought to play, and how you might start to play.

When I was a child:

My favorite playtime activities were _____

I had a talent for _____

I was afraid to _____

I always wanted to _____

In this current chapter that is now passing away:

My favorite creative activities have been _____

I have a talent for _____

I have been afraid to _____

I have been wanting to _____

In this next chapter:

I will creatively explore _____

I will try my talent for _____

I will have the courage to _____

I will try _____

TO SUM UP

Laughter is the best medicine, right? So creating a space to play, a space with no rules or limits on your smiles or ingenuity, makes for a happy home. Set aside room for play and inspired activity, space that feels safe and allows family members to explore new creative habits. When you welcome spontaneity, you also encourage growth.

Chapter 12.
Happy and Achieving: Advancing Your Career and Education

"Growth is never by mere chance; it is
the result of forces working together."
—James Cash Penney

THERE ARE TIMES IN LIFE WHEN YOU HAVE to make a big, bold move in your education or career. Sometimes it's because a life transition, like perhaps a divorce, demands that you take on a new role. Sometimes it's because you sense a calling within you, a deep and urgent need to change, learn, and grow. Regardless of what compels the shift, when it's time to learn something new, your home can be a big help in the process, or it can really get in your way.

Taking on a new career or course of study might mean that you need a quiet place to work. It might mean that you need a room where you can talk privately on the phone with clients. It might mean that you need a closet and bathroom space where you can quickly get ready each morning without waking up the rest of your household.

The space of a professional, career-minded person is easy to spot. It feels focused, successful, even powerful. That kind of space changes the behavior of both the professional person who works there and the clients and workers who enter it. If you are contemplating growing into a new professional role, consider creating a space that already looks like the success you plan to achieve. If you start each day by walking into the office of a successful, career-minded woman, you are much more likely to conduct yourself like a successful woman, and the world will respond to you that way. You will be your own self-fulfilling prophecy. But it works in reverse too. If every day you walk into an office that looks like it's occupied by a lazy, disorganized, discouraged worker, you will see yourself that way, and the universe will treat you as such.

You've heard the expression "Dress for the job you want." Whether you are just starting a new job or you are decades into a career, the idea is to wear the "uniform" of the person you aspire to be, not the outfit of the position you want to leave behind. Imagine showing up to your new job at Subway wearing a McDonald's uniform. You'd look either confused or silly or both. Naturally that wouldn't happen, but working in a space that is incongruent with your goals is just as foolish.

Of course, that doesn't mean that an administrative assistant should come to work in the same three-piece Armani suit as the top lawyer at her firm, but, if she's seeking a higher position within the company, she should wear an ensemble that suggests she's capable, professional, and trustworthy. The entry-level lawyer, on the other hand, might want to start investing in the expected attire of an established lawyer. Unfortunately, humans *do* judge capability by image (aka, we do judge a book by its cover). You can fight that system, or use it to your advantage.

The same logic applies to the home or home office. Aspiring to make $10,000 per month doesn't mean you should immediately embark on a $100,000 kitchen remodel, but it does mean you should be living and working in a space that feels future-focused and successful to you. How we dress our home can have as great an impact on our upward mobility as how we dress ourselves. If you have to make a budgetary choice between aligning your wardrobe or aligning your home with your career aspirations, I suggest addressing the wardrobe first, since you carry that image with you into the world. But don't wait too long on the home improvements, because that is the space that helps *you believe* that your successful future and positive outcomes are imminent.

You might be thinking that this chapter is meant for the work-from-home entrepreneur. Yes, the most obvious connection between career and home is for the at-home worker, but the home also absolutely impacts the success of any nine-to-fiver. How you feel when you walk in your door after work, or when you wake up and get ready in the morning, affects your self-worth and how you expect people to relate to you in your professional world. When you look around your home, do you see the home of a self-assured, confident person in charge of her destiny and success? Or is your home, and are you, controlled by circumstances that feel out of your influence? How would you feel if a coworker or your boss were to drop by your home unannounced?

How you feel when you wake up and get ready in the morning affects your self-worth and how you expect people to relate to you in your professional life.

If your home feels cluttered, naked, or uninviting, that means you leave the house each day with less certainty and conviction than you would if you woke up in a home that felt warm, personal, and thoughtful. While "warm, personal, and thoughtful" might have different meanings to different people, the key is to discover what it means for you and make it a reality in your home.

Remember James, my client from Chapter 6 who'd been depressed because of his job loss? It turned out that the makeover we did in their living room gave James the momentum he needed to make positive life changes. Instead of carrying that feeling of shame with him as he looked for work, he carried a sense of hope and pride.

Along with the living room makeover, however, we also made over James' and Leslie's home office. Over time it had become more of a storage room, filled with boxes, stacks of paper, and half-finished projects. When James had been employed, that storage-room ambiance didn't bother him too much, but once he lost his job he felt trapped in a house that embarrassed him. And he also had no place where he could work on sending out resumes or strategizing his next career move.

Together we reclaimed the office and created a calm, inspiring workspace. By the end of the project, he had decided that instead of working for someone else again, he was ready and able to start his own business. By changing his home, James changed his outlook. We created space for hope and for dreaming. Changing this home changed the way this budding entrepreneur interacted with the entire world.

READY TO LAUNCH?

Do you have career advancement in mind? Do you picture a bright future for yourself? How committed are you to that new path? If you are surrounded by the stuff of your old life, it's going to be much harder to launch a new adventure. If you are *saying* that you want the new, exciting, scary thing but you are holding on tightly to the security of old habits, then the universe is going to let you keep the old ways. It will respond to your actions, not your words.

In *The Power of Place*, Winifred Gallagher describes a study of college students in which researchers found that "the best indication of which students were likeliest to drop out of college was the décor of their dorm rooms during freshman year; the kids who embellished them lavishly and included local touches, such as university posters, were far more apt to stick it out than those who made little effort or decked their rooms with hometown memorabilia, say, a dried corsage from the high school prom." How crazy is that? A new college friend could walk into your freshman dorm room and instantly know how likely it was that you'd be making it through to graduation, just by seeing how connected you were to your future versus your past.

If you really want to propel forward, allow the old you to make way for the new you. It's hard to stride ahead confidently while you're carrying a bunch of old baggage. You need those hands free to grab opportunities! Does that mean you have to throw everything out and start over? Of course not. But you benefit by taking an honest look at your life and your home and by seeing the true messages you are sending yourself. When we are stuck in the past, complaining about missed opportunities, gazing at high school trophies and wishing for the good ol' days, surrounding ourselves with the relics of old relationships, old jobs, old stories, mourning the past and what is lost, we never really move on from it and, therefore, we never truly embrace our next chapter. You have to let go of what *was* in order to bring in what *will be*.

**You have to let go of what was
in order to bring in what will be.**

It's not just at home where this inventory has to happen; it's at work too. If you work in an office or a cubicle, look around. What does it say about the person who works there? Are there photos of your kids from a decade ago? Are there strings of beads and party hats from the office party from several years past? Is the plant in the corner nearly dead? Those are not signs of a person motivated and thriving; they are signs of a person complacent about the current situation and nostalgically connected to the past.

Bear in mind that there is nothing inherently wrong with being comfortable in the now and displaying reminders of good memories. If you are living your dream life, happy with your relationships, health, income, and other markers of success, then by no means do you need to change anything. But if you picked up this book, I suspect you are reaching for something more fulfilling than the status quo.

You don't have to eliminate the family pictures; just update the photos and be inspired by what your kids are up to *now*. Toss the old party favors and make room for the next social event, maybe even getting involved in the planning. Get rid of the dying plant and either bring one in that can thrive or don't have a plant at all. (Peace lilies are one of my favorites—I have yet to kill one.) Having *no* plant is better than having a dead plant, and also better than having a silk plant covered in dust. (Don't get me started on sad silk trees in too-small rattan pots with their little covering of crumbling moss.)

THE ENVIRONMENT OF THE ENTREPRENEUR

Of course, nowhere does the home environment have a more potent impact on a career than for the work-from-home businessperson. My colleague and friend Stacy Erickson, owner of Home Key Organization, made over her home office and immediately doubled her business. Was that because her new space allowed her to concentrate better? Was it because she exuded renewed strength and success, and her clients responded to that new energy? Probably both. Whatever the reason, changing your space has a nearly magical power, one that often amazes even those of us who work in the field of home design.

WHAT IF CLIENTS NEVER SEE YOUR SPACE?

Many entrepreneurs work from home and no one else ever sees their workspace. Does it really matter what it looks like? Absolutely! Let's take, for instance, your office chair. If it is uncomfortable, shabby, and doesn't promote good posture, your clients *will hear that* when you speak with them on the phone. What? Really? *Yes!* Try recording your voicemail message in two ways. First, record the message sitting slouched on a squishy chair, and don't smile. Listen to the recording and note the energy in your voice. Then record the same message sitting or even standing with excellent posture, and smile. Listen to the alternative—you might be surprised by how much more alive, capable, and happy the second message sounds.

Take some simple steps to boost the mood in your workspace. Be sure the furniture helps you sit comfortably and properly. Modify the layout so you can easily access what you need. Freshen up the design to make you feel happy and successful so that clients can hear the smile in your voice.

Some people hang inspirational art or photos above their desks (their kids, a desired vacation destination, some representation of a financial goal) to remind them why they work so hard. That can be great, but make sure your art inspires action rather than a wistfulness or distraction from the task at hand. Make sure the pictures of your kids are up-to-date. Surround yourself with reminders of your reachable stretch goals.

Regularly refresh your workspace, perhaps every six months or so. That doesn't mean you have to completely redecorate your space, but repot the plant in a new container, or take down the holiday cards and put up new family pictures. Even just a good cleaning—getting all the dust that has settled behind your computer—can do it. We stop seeing the things in front of us that do not change, but their impact doesn't go away. We end up with lampshades covered in thick layers of dust, not because we are bad, neglectful people but because we're just busy and become blind to our own spaces. Nonetheless, that thick layer of dust sends a pretty powerful message that you are running on a treadmill of futility.

CLIENT CONSIDERATIONS: WHEN PEOPLE *ARE* GOING TO VISIT YOUR SPACE

What if you *do* have clients come to your office? Whether you work out of a home office or an outside office, the importance of your space just jumped to a whole new level. I have walked into accountants' offices and been greeted by forests of paper piles topped with empty coffee cups and grimy walls with a single too-small print hanging askew behind the desk. You get the picture. The person may be the world's most brilliant accountant, but the space suggests that he or she is unable to manage the work and makes me question whether deadlines are met and details are addressed. Is that fair? It doesn't matter if it's fair. As I said earlier, we *do judge people by how they look and what they surround themselves with.* So whether you like it or not, potential clients will assess you by your office as well as your clothes, physical fitness, voice, hygiene, and smile.

Be intentional with your space. And if creating a space that is professional and inviting is not your talent, or if you simply do not have time to do the work, hire it out. That is why there are experts in every field. I have no business doing my own taxes. Sure, I could figure it out, but what a waste of my natural talents, time, and passions. Likewise, maybe you can figure out your office space, but it might just be a waste of your time and talents. Collaborating with a designer will likely get you a better end result: an office that helps you focus on what you do best.

DELEGATE FOR SUCCESS

Apparently the idea of having the person who is best at a job actually *do* that job is an established economic principle. In their book *It's Not You, It's the Dishes* (formerly *Spousonomics*), authors Paula Szuchman and Jenny Anderson apply this concept to marriage. They lay out the principle that work should not be divided fifty-fifty in a relationship, but rather that work should be divided by talent and interest. For example, my husband is a great cook. I am a great housekeeper. He cooks; I clean. Simple as that. We could, out of a sense of "fairness," each do 50 percent of the cooking and cleaning, but then we'd both be miserable half the time.

Why do I bring all this up? Because there are people who might tell you that hiring help to decorate your space is foolish. But if you understand that your space will have an emotional and economic impact on the success of your company, *and* if you recognize that decorating and space planning is not your forte, hiring a pro isn't foolish: it's a brilliant use of your precious resources of time and money.

IS A HOME OFFICE RIGHT FOR YOU?

If you run a business (either from your home or from a separate location) and you host clients, you absolutely must create a space that feels professional and *safe*. We know that first impressions are essential, and a bad first impression may be your only impression. If you're deciding whether to have a home or an outside office, look at it from two perspectives: yours and your clients'.

I recently consulted with a life coach who was setting up a home office. He had planned to use the top level of his three-story town home for the office. It had the best light and a nice layout. During my consultation I asked him whether he anticipated having female clients (yes) and then pointed out the obvious: female clients might not feel all *that* comfortable traipsing through a single guy's private home, up three levels, to the farthest point from the front door. I suggested he use the lowest-level room for his office—it not only had a bathroom nearby but was also located right next to the front door and had French doors that opened onto a back patio. This change created an experience that was more professional and more comfortable for the client.

When planning your office space, think about how it will affect your clients.

When planning your office space, think about the impression it will make on your clients and any anxieties clients may be bringing into a meeting. This might be especially obvious if you work as a massage therapist or PTSD counselor, but it is just as important for the accountant and the personal trainer. Consider the location of the space in your home relative to safety (both yours and the clients), to distractions from family members and pets, and to comfort. Also consider the geography of your home and neighborhood: How will clients enter the home? Where will they park? Many small businesses are run from the home, but the most *successful* small businesses put a lot of thought and intention behind the space itself and the client experience.

CLUTTERED DESK, CLUTTERED MIND?

I'm often asked, "Does a cluttered desk matter?"

In a 2013 study, Kathleen Vohs, PhD, of the University of Minnesota Carlson School of Management, found that working in a messy room seems to help people try new things and come up with creative ideas. In referencing Vohs's experiment and keying in on the suggestion that messiness may be linked to creativity, author Randa Goode wrote this: "If that is the case, when it comes to my desk and writing, then I may be the most creative person in the world. Heck, maybe in the universe."

So clutter may enhance your creativity. On the other hand, psychologists Darby Saxbe and Rena Repetti published a study showing that clutter is more than just an annoyance. They studied the cortisol (stress-indicating hormone) levels of people who described their homes as messy or cluttered, and found that those living in what they perceived to be cluttered environments actually experienced higher rates of depressed mood toward evening. Their findings suggest that we can link what we call "stressful" house environments with psychological responses that can markedly compromise homeowner health. Constant clutter can create situational depression and compromise your long-term well-being.

What do these study results mean for you? It's simple: consider *your own needs* when you answer the question about whether that cluttered desk is keeping you from doing your best work. The right amount of clutter can boost your creativity. The wrong amount of clutter can elevate your stress. And stress not only hurts your creativity in the short term, it hurts your health in the long term.

The right amount of clutter can boost your creativity. The wrong amount can elevate your stress.

When asked about clutter in media interviews, I find that the interviewer usually has a bias. Messy people ask with the *hope* that they don't have to go home and tidy up, and tidy people ask it with an air of knowingness, just *certain* that I'll back up their assertion that cleanliness is next to godliness. In the end, I don't think there is one right answer. My own habit is that during a project, whether designing a living room, writing a book, or getting ready for a party, I create chaos and stacks and piles galore. I start with a pristine work area, devolve into utter chaos complete with two-day-old dishes, and after I wrap up the project, return to a perfectly tidy state. That is my way.

If the chaos stage of my creative work goes on for too long, or if my work hours are so long that I have neglected the rest of my home to the point of disarray, I'm known to have cleaning emergencies. This also happens if I am really, truly stuck on a problem at work and feel like I am just beating my head against the wall, unable to find a solution. In *House as a Mirror of Self*, Clare Cooper Marcus writes, "One way in which most of us are aware of the almost membrane-like connection between self and environment is when things somehow get 'out of control' and we feel disordered in ourselves. Who hasn't had the experience of tidying a cluttered desk and subsequently feeling more able to think straight? Of cleaning out stuff from an attic or storeroom and feeling a great sense of accomplishment, or perhaps a feeling of being more in control?" We all have different sensitivities to clutter, and our job is to figure out our own tolerance for clutter and, of course, balance that with the impression of stability and professionalism we want to give our clients.

DO YOU *REALLY* KNOW WHAT'S IN THOSE PILES?

Even if you have a high tolerance for clutter, that disorder can turn into a burden if left unchecked. Can you *really* find what you need, when you need it? It's all a matter of honest evaluation, and sometimes we have to shake things up and try something new to see if our habits are serving us. Author Winifred Gallagher writes, "One reason we work so hard to keep our surroundings predictable is that we rely on them to help us segue smoothly from role to role throughout the day." If you need that messy desk to get you into the role of entrepreneur, who am I to ask you to change it? But if that same messy desk is actually a source of confusion, frustration, embarrassment, or procrastination, then of course you should change it.

Despite all the how-to books out there on getting perfectly organized, there is no one answer, and it does take commitment and work. That is why it's helpful to first connect with the reason *why* you are going to make some changes, and keep that front and center as you change your habits or your space. Knowing *why* helps you determine if your space just needs organizing and a fresh coat of paint, whether it needs new furniture and some built-in storage, or if it is time to invest in an office away from home. Without that touchstone, you won't end up with the results you need, and you'll have likely wasted precious time and money. The exercises at the end of this chapter should help create clarity around your *why* and give you some tools for success too.

Activity 39. Setting the Scene for Success

What does success look and feel like for you? In this exercise we'll explore that question and identify where your existing space might not be meeting your needs.

1. Write down your career or education goal: _____
2. Identify a mentor or role model in that field: _____
3. Use your imagination to think of what your mentor's or role model's work-space might look like. What kind of chair might they have? Desk? What books line their shelves?

How I imagine my mentor's workspace to be: _____

_____

_____

_____

_____

_____

_____

4. Now look at your workspace and, as if you did not work there, describe the person who works there. Based only on what you see, what do they do? What are their strengths, and what are their weaknesses? Judge as objectively as you can. Is this someone you would trust with your money? Is this the office of a successful person in your field?

My workspace looks like the workspace of someone who: _____

_____

_____

_____

_____

_____

_____

5. Based on your answers to the above, and the alignment between how you imagine your mentor might work and live and how you are currently working and living, create an action list of three powerful changes you could make to your space, and the differences these changes will make:

Task/Action to take	Difference it would make
1. _____	_____
2. _____	_____
3. _____	_____

After you identify three actions, mark on your calendar dates by which you will accomplish each action and how you will get it done. By each action, note resources you'll need to get it done.

Activity 40. Now and Later
In this activity, let's identify where you are emotionally and physically in your work life, and where you would like to be. Fill out each blank with descriptive words that fit how you feel now, and how you wish to feel.

At work now:
I feel _____
It feels _____
My chair is _____
Starting a project feels _____
Finishing a project feels _____
The place where I take a break is _____
When I answer a phone call I _____
When I get stuck I _____
My computer is _____
I share my space with _____
I wish I could _____
When I reach for something I need it is _____

At work later:
I will feel _____
It will feel _____
My chair will be _____
Starting a project will feel _____
Finishing a project will feel _____
The place where I take a break will be _____
When I answer a phone call I will _____
When I get stuck I will _____

My computer will be _____
I will share my space with _____
I will be able to _____
When I reach for something I need it will be _____

Read your answers and note three important discrepancies between your at-work now and at-work later descriptions:

     1. _____
     2. _____
     3. _____

Now, most importantly, identify how things will change after you modify the space. Take a few minutes and imagine how you will feel, what you will accomplish, and what success will feel like when you are working in a space that supports you. Really feel it, taste it, touch it, listen to it. What does the floor feel like under your feet? What scents fill the air? What snacks are on hand to nourish you? What colors surround you? (Note: For a guide to visualizing your new workspace, visit happystartsathome.com and try "Put the Om in Your Home," a twenty-minute guided meditation.)

After I commit to changing my workspace, I will:

_____
_____
_____
_____

Note: This can be a great group exercise to do with your employees too. Have each person fill it out independently, and then discuss one-on-one or in a group, depending on the personality of your company and staff.

Activity 41. Working from Home: An Entrepreneurial Map

Create a basic floor plan of your home. It doesn't matter if it's done to scale. Just be sure each area is represented, including storage spaces like closets and garages and outside spaces like decks and gardens. Choose three pencil, marker, or crayon colors.

Once you have drafted your floor plan, mark your dedicated workspace in one color. Mark areas where you work but that are shared with other activities in a second color. Mark areas of your home that you use during your workday that are unrelated to work. This might include the laundry room, the kitchen, the front entry, even your kids' rooms if you find yourself tidying up during your workday. Be honest about which spaces are truly dedicated to your work, which are shared, and which are unrelated to work but definitely fill part of your workday routine.

Look over the map. Are you surprised by which areas feel productive and dedicated and which areas feel distracting? Take a moment to write about your mapping experience:

_____

_____

_____

_____

_____

_____

_____

TO SUM UP

The reason advertising works so well is that it is nearly impossible to resist believing a message we see and hear over and over again. If your work environment is telling you that you are lazy, lacking in success and talent, and undeserving of a supportive space, you are unconsciously creating an obstacle that will make it that much harder to achieve the success you are capable of.

Creating a successful space doesn't mean you have to invest in a $10,000 mahogany desk. *Successful doesn't equal expensive.* In fact, most of my entrepreneurial clients have built their space primarily from Ikea. Rather than focusing on spending, put your efforts into creating an *intentional* space, carefully considering color and layout.

A successful space doesn't have to mimic a gentleman's club library or a slick Silicon Valley interior complete with a rope swing and Ping-Pong table. There is no certain look to success. That look and feeling should be guided by your brand, your work, your clients' needs and expectations, and your own needs, whether that's calm energy, beautiful colors, or inspirational views.

Both your office and your home (and especially your home office) should reflect the success you have already enjoyed and the success you will go on to achieve in your career. Your workspace is an essential tool that can help you climb your personal ladder of success.

Chapter 13.
Happy in Your Spiritual Home:
Living Your Visible Values

> "The spiritual quest is not some added
> benefit to our life, something you embark
> on if you have the time and inclination. We
> are spiritual beings on an earthly journey.
> Our spirituality makes up our beingness."
> —John Bradshaw

WHAT DOES IT MEAN TO HAVE A SPIRITUAL HOME? Is it a home that hosts Bible studies? A home where you meditate daily? A home with corner shrines? It could be any of these things and still not actually be a spiritual home. It could be none of these things and yet be a deeply spiritual home.

If there is no one way to create a spiritual home, how do you make sure that your home is meeting your spiritual needs? As you've done with all of the other slices of life, identify what spirituality means to you, how you need to be supported in your faith, and what needs to change in your home to do that.

Sometimes our spiritual lives seem to be experienced only in a church or at a retreat. Let's invite that spirituality into our homes. I have experienced spiritual renewal everywhere from my childhood church in suburban Michigan to a silent meditation retreat in the middle of a Pacific Northwest rainforest. Each time, though, my connection to spirit seems to fade as I reenter "real life" and face the chaos of balancing the work, housekeeping, and relationships in my life. Can you relate to that struggle?

How can you bring the meditation retreat home? How can you make sure that your spiritual needs are met in your home so that you are constantly in touch with what deeply matters to you? If we accept that your spirituality is an essential thread in the fabric of your life, then naturally we need to make sure it is represented in your home and that your faith is supported and nurtured.

Spirituality at home has three components: what you have, what you do not have, and what you do.

STUFF VERSUS SPIRITUAL TOUCHSTONES: WHAT DO YOU HAVE IN YOUR HOME?

"Be grateful for the home you have, knowing that at this moment, all you have is all you need."
—Sarah Ban Breathnach

Creating a spiritual home is less about *things* and more about space—to breathe. To be. To pray. Do you have space in your home where you can practice your faith?

For some people, a spiritual home means literally having an altar or meditation space. Such spaces help clear the mind and ease worship or reflection. Research shows that as little as three minutes a day of meditation has great power, so why not create a space that helps you focus? Something as small as a smooth rock, or as large as a whole guest room turned into a meditation space, can support you in resting your mind and letting things flow again. My client Monica had a lovely, airy, rarely used guest bedroom. What she really needed was a space where, after a long, hectic day in her medical practice, she could quiet her mind and reconnect with the meaningful things in her life. We made over the room with a lovely daybed so it could double as a guest and meditation room.

Since we can't always closet ourselves away when we need to get in touch with our faith, a spiritual home doesn't just have special spaces for prayer and meditation. It also allows you to connect with what is meaningful while doing even the most mundane stuff like cleaning the cat box or making the bed.

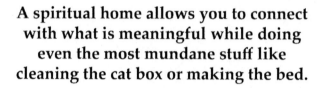

**A spiritual home allows you to connect
with what is meaningful while doing
even the most mundane stuff like
cleaning the cat box or making the bed.**

The Shakers, as a people, knew that the sights, sounds, and smells of a spiritual home needed to resonate with a connection to Spirit, and for them that meant filling their homes with light. Their architectural and color choices were all about bringing light into interior environments, meant to give a taste of heaven. "Good and evil are typified by light and darkness," wrote Shaker elder Aurelia Mace. "Therefore, if we bring light into a dark room, the darkness disappears, and inasmuch as a soul is filled with good, evil will disappear."

As you think about your home, perhaps you want to set up a specific meditation or prayer space, but consider the big picture of your home too. It's possible to create harmony between your spiritual needs and your living spaces. Make sure that what you value is seen and reflected as you look around your home. Many of my Christian clients display beautiful crosses. Many of my Buddhist clients have altars. One symbol of your faith, however, can't counter a house full of items that show a contradictory set of values. If you say that your deepest values center on nature but your home is over-filled with low-quality, rarely used stuff, does that align with your values? If you say that your deepest values center on family and connection with others, but your whole home is focused on TV and screen time, does that align with your values? If your God is a god of lovingkindness, simplicity, and generosity, do you see that in your home?

If you connect to Spirit by being surrounded by friends and family, it is essential to set up a home that makes it easy to gather and entices people to linger. If you connect to Spirit by retreating into silence and prayer, set aside a private, sacred spot. And if you connect by surrounding yourself with nature, make sure you have easy access to the outdoors.

WHAT SHOULD LEAVE YOUR HOME?

"This is what happens when we let go of things: we step out of our own reality and into God's." —Allison Vesterfelt

Creating a spiritual home is as much about what you *do not* have as it is about what you do have. Perhaps more so.

Our lives are, quite frankly, overstimulating. There is too much noise, too many options, too much input for us to hear the voice of our conscience, of our instincts, or of God. The only way we know to cope is to tune out and turn off. We know we pay a price in the quantity and quality of our experiences and miss opportunities to connect socially, but with such relentless stimulation attacking us, it's as if we have no choice. We shut down just so we don't implode.

We tune out in response to the overstimulation of our outside environments, yet then we turn around and compound that with overstimulation at home. Junk mail, kids' toys, television, radio, newspapers, cell phones, email . . . It's no wonder we can't hear our own inner voice or the voice of the universe. We must create space for silence, for retreat, and for calm. What better place to do that than in the place you call home?

That means we probably have to let go of a bunch of stuff. We have to stop hoarding. And hoarding may not look quite like what you imagine. Hoarders are not just those poor souls on TV who are barricaded inside their own homes with decades of trash or two-for-one purchases. Hoarding is found in every ungenerous choice we make. It shows up every time we stuff yet another lidless piece of Tupperware in the already-crowded cabinet. It is found when we keep hundreds of childhood art pieces from now-grown children. It is found when we refuse to create space for our partner's preferences. Every time we are ungenerous we are lacking in faith, because faith permits us to let go and know that we have and will have everything we need.

Faith permits us to let go of worry and know that we have, and will have, everything we need.

Creating a spiritual home means letting go of the stories we tell ourselves, like "I don't have enough." "I am always broke." "I don't know what's going to come; better to be safe than sorry." As Marianne Williamson says in *The Law of Divine Compensation*, "Spiritual growth involves giving up the stories of your past so the universe can write a new one."

One day as I was sitting in a café writing this book, I thought it might be nice to take home one of the fantastic banana cream pies the café is famous for. I knew that the café preferred twenty-four-hour notice for whole-pie orders, so I told the waitress not to worry if they didn't have one to sell. She said she thought they actually did. A few minutes later she came back and said, "The owners don't know how busy we'll be tomorrow, so they don't want to sell what we have today."

What a poignant statement of fear! I think it sums up so much of what we carry—in our purses, in our homes, and in our minds. In that moment the café managers could have sold a whole pie but instead, out of fear, they held on to the pie. I understand not wanting to disappoint tomorrow's customers, and I didn't mind going home pieless, but at the same time, anything can happen. I mean, a freak overnight December snowstorm *could* have shut down the city that night and the whole pie *could* have gone bad. Who knows? Why hold on to something now *just in case* you need it, when you can give it to someone who needs it and to whom it will bring joy now? Why not have enough faith to be generous today, and trust that the universe will provide for you tomorrow?

You may be familiar with this verse: "Look at the birds in the sky: They do not sow, or reap, or gather into barns, yet your heavenly Father feeds them" (Matthew 6:26). The underlying tenet of nearly every faith is that we will be cared for, that there is enough to go around, that we can trust in abundance. Look to your faith as you make decisions about what should be in your home.

WHAT WE SEE, WE BELIEVE

"You can't hear God when your mind is crowded with thoughts, worries, fears, and plans, or if you always have the radio or TV on. And if you constantly have your phone against your ear, when God calls all he gets is a busy signal!"
—Rick Warren

It is so easy to live in a state of fear. Our culture, especially the media, bombards us with *Buy now! Act now! Don't miss this show tonight!* Try turning down the volume on all those messages (maybe by turning off the screens in your home?) and listening for the voice of God in your home and in your life.

What we have in our homes speaks to our values and reinforces those values. So if you are surrounding yourself with messages that are counter to your core values, you are likely to act on the messages that permeate your home, not necessarily the values you *wish* you followed. That's how advertising works, of course. There you are, watching a favorite TV show, with not a single thought about Oreos. Then *bam!* There it is, Oreo porn right in front of you, all black and white and perfect. Suddenly, you want an Oreo (or insert your own guilty pleasure here).

That is how the whole keeping-up-with-the-Joneses thing works too. You're living a contented life, snug in your home with your cat and your cup of tea, and then some sexy actor comes on the television, suggesting that if you eat *this* yogurt, buy *this* car, you will be happier/sexier/richer. You may be savvy enough to dismiss that message the first time, but after you see and hear it over and over and over again, you simply do not have the mental capacity to stop the barrage. The invaders get in and you start questioning your status, jealous of what others have, and uncertain that what you have is enough. And whether you have twenty dollars to your name or you are a multibillionaire, it works the same, and you will feel the push for *more, more, more.*

In *The Secret*, Rhonda Byrne says, "If we want to see different pictures on our television, we change the channel and tune into a new frequency." She is talking about shifting your thoughts in order to see new things in your life. So, where is your home leading your thoughts? If you want to change your thoughts, why not change the pictures around you and create a whole new channel?

WHAT DO YOU DO IN YOUR HOME?

"Zen does not confuse spirituality with thinking about God while one is peeling potatoes. Zen spirituality is just to peel the potatoes." —Alan Watts

Your home is the foundation of everything in your life—including your faith.

Compare the tenets of your faith to the behavior going on in your home and in your heart. Do you wish to practice forgiveness, but find yourself wallowing in anger at your ex instead of letting the past be the past? Look around. If reminders of your past relationship surround you and keep you tied to old hurts, you will find it hard to let go. It's hard enough to release past injuries, but so much harder to practice forgiveness if you are surrounded by pain. But if you create a space that allows you to move on, you'll find that you can more easily practice forgiveness because you are able to look forward instead of backward. In *You Can Heal Your Life*, Louise Hay writes, "Many people come to me and say they cannot enjoy today because of something that happened in the past." Many of us hold tightly to our past in large part because *it feels good to have that past to blame*. But if you want to fully align with your spiritual self, you'd do well to let go visually, physically, and emotionally.

Do you wish to practice kindness and consideration? Take a look at the activities and games in your home. Are they all screen-focused or solo-play games? Consider making your main areas screen-free and choosing games that encourage teamwork and sharing. By having to interact and to negotiate, we learn to accommodate other people's needs and to practice being considerate. What we play, we learn, and it influences our behavior outside the home.

Do you wish to practice generosity? Look at your belongings and consider how much comes in versus how much goes out. A simple one-in, one-out rule can help you balance giving and receiving. It can apply to shoes, games, coats, even relationships and money. To fully commit yourself to a new partner, it is important to release the baggage of old relationships and let the new relationship grow on its own foundation. And when it comes to money, the simple principle of tithing reminds you that 10 percent of what you receive is meant to be given back.

Do you wish to practice gratitude? Gratitude is a central tenet of prayer, especially before meals. If your busy home and lifestyle prevent your family from gathering around the table to celebrate a meal and show gratitude for the bounty, a change might be in order.

These small, incremental changes are like drops in a bucket, and over time, you'll find your bucket full. Just celebrating your faith and values as a family one more time a week than before means you are growing in alignment with your faith. In time it will come more naturally and you will come to crave that time with the calm and support of the universe.

LEAVE ROOM FOR SPIRITUAL GROWTH

"The measure of intelligence is the ability to change." —Albert Einstein

Setting up a spiritual home isn't a one-time event. Spiritual homes are not stagnant. That is because what you need from your home, and in your home, will change over time. The systems that worked for you five years ago might not work for you now. How has your life changed in the last decade? New job? New family? New hobbies? New friends? Unexpected health challenges? As input and demands shift, you'll want to adjust your home to meet your new needs.

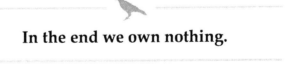

In the end we own nothing.

Finally, the spiritual home reminds us that in the end we own nothing. Our connection to the otherworldly has nothing to do with our sofas, cars, or TVs. In *You Can Heal Your Life*, author Louise Hay reminds us to enjoy today: "We do not own anything. We only use possessions for a period of time until they pass on to someone else. Sometimes a possession may stay in a family for a few generations, but eventually it will pass on. There is a natural rhythm and flow of life. Things come, and things go. I believe that when something goes, it is only to make room for something new and better."

Activity 42. Values as Seen by Strangers

It can be difficult to see our own homes objectively. If you can, do this exercise with a friend. Ask your friend to imagine that she's never visited your home before. Ask her to walk through, room by room, and write down three values that she thinks the family living there holds. What do they cherish? Honor? Worship? Crave? What do they devalue? What is neglected? Dismissed? If your friend is open to it, reverse roles and do the same for her. Walking through her home and identifying values can be just as instructive.

Look over the list. Are you surprised by the values that seem to be reflected in your home? Take a moment to journal on your experience, seeing your home with fresh eyes, and answer this question: Does my home align with my spiritual and value needs?

_____

_____

_____

_____

_____

_____

Activity 43. Bless (Instead of Curse) Your Home

Pressing the garage-door remote, turning the key in your lock, preheating the oven for dinner, throwing laundry into the washer—these can all be spiritual practices. They are opportunities to express gratitude for the blessings in your life: your home, the food on your table, the convenience of at-home laundry equipment. Often, however, instead of expressing gratitude, we unconsciously invoke a curse. Our habits are daily practices. Are you willing to continue practicing frustration, ingratitude, and entitlement, or is it time to start a practice of gratitude, generosity, and kindness?

Think of your daily routine at home. Identify three generally frustrating moments in your day. Examples are a sticky door, a spouse who leaves the lights on, or a kid who forgets to put the milk back in the fridge. Identify three at-home frustrations:

1. _____

2. _____

3. _____

Pick one of the three and put a sticky note somewhere near where the incident occurs. Write a word that will trigger the opposite reaction from your normal reaction. For example, if your usual reaction is anger when your daughter leaves the milk out, write "love." If it is frustration, write "gratitude." If it is anxiety, write "protected." For seven days, use every sticky-note encounter to flip your words. Instead of saying something like, "Ugh, why can't she remember to put the damn milk away?" say, "I am so grateful that my daughter made herself breakfast and went off to school on time and is healthy." It's okay if you say the frustrated thing first; it's hard to change your mindset immediately. But as soon as you see the sticky note, say the opposite, even if you are not feeling it (yet).

Do this activity for three weeks, adding one frustration each week. By the end of the practice you will naturally look for the blessing rather than react in frustration.

Activity 44. Love Letters

Even with its flaws, a home is a blessing. For the next thirty days, keep a journal of love letters to your home. Recognize and appreciate what you have, rather than focus on the long list of everything that needs to get done. Write at least one full page of gratitudes, large and small, for the things in your home. Here are journal examples:

> *Thank you for hot showers. Thank you for a roof over my head. Thank you for east-facing windows that let in morning light. Thank you for a room for each of my kids. Thank you for flushing toilets. Thank you for a dishwasher . . .*

If you have been practicing negativity lately, you may find this exercise surprisingly hard at first, but stay with it. Yes, frustrations exist, but for five minutes of the morning, choose to ignore those frustrations while you write the love letter to your home.

There is no magic to the words—the magic is in the practice. Focus on what you have rather than what you do not have. Is there anything more spiritual?

Activity 45. Eliminating Distractions

This one is a toughy. Are you *actually* committed to having a spiritual home? It may be time to unplug (gasp!). You are in control here, and only you know the biggest distractions that keep you from having open communication with God. For me, busyness is one big distraction. TV is another. The radio in the car is a third. And food is a fourth.

Think through your day and identify the top three distractions that keep you from having more conversations with God. The things you do in moments of weakness to feel better, when perhaps it would have been better to draw directly from the Well. Identify your top three distractions:

1. _____
2. _____
3. _____

Pick one of the three and commit to a day, a week, or a month without that distraction. You are in charge here, and only you can identify the achievable challenge that is right for you. When you are halfway through the period of eliminating distraction #1, add distraction #2. When you are halfway through the period of eliminating distraction #2, add distraction #3. Try to do the morning writing exercise (Activity 44, Love Letters) in tandem with this exercise. The love letters will help you keep your commitment to clearing distractions and listening for God's lead throughout the day.

TO SUM UP

Building a spiritual home begins with identifying the foundational values of your faith, and then looking honestly at your home to see if it reflects and supports those values. No matter what you need in life, if you align your home with those needs—spiritually, physically, and emotionally—you will find it easier to live a congruent, easy, and happy life.

Your home doesn't have to be perfect. As Suzy Chiazzari writes in *Our Place*, "Learning to accept a home that is not perfect is like learning to live with another person. You have to accept his or her good and bad traits, and create a space where you can both feel good without compromising each other." That is part of the spiritual journey too. Understanding that the world is bigger than just ourselves. Understanding that we get to accommodate others, and they get to accommodate us.

I am not here to tell you what values to follow, just to ask if you are living in alignment with your faith, and whether your home reflects your values.

Chapter 14.
Happy with Yourself:
Enjoying Strong Self-Worth

"First we shape our dwellings. Then our dwellings shape us." —Winston Churchill

THIS CHAPTER IS ABOUT BOUNDARIES. Creating healthy boundaries around whom and what you let into your life, and to which voices you are willing to listen. About ignoring or embracing trends, and permitting change over time. The walls and mirrors of your home reflect your self-worth and self-image and send an inescapable message about what you feel you deserve and your place in this world.

A home that reflects a high level of self-worth is not necessarily one filled with expensive, fancy furnishings. Likewise, a home filled with secondhand furniture and Craigslist finds doesn't necessarily reflect a low self-image. I have found no correlation between cost of furnishings and happiness. I have noticed other correlations, however.

Indications of low self-worth:

- Too many belongings
- Dust on all the belongings
- Lack of pictures or art
- Broken things
- Unpacked boxes
- Inherited paint colors, especially from ex-partners
- Dirty walls
- Museum-perfect spaces

- Offices that have become storage rooms
- Naked bedrooms
- All rooms overrun with kid toys
- Dangerous furniture (like glass-cornered coffee tables)

These are warning flags that cause me to wonder: Is the person who lives here taking care of her soul?

As you examine how your home reflects your self-worth, your home's entry is a wonderful place to start. Let's try this: I'll describe two of my clients' entries, both their public and their for-family-use-only doorways, and you think about how you'd feel approaching each entry. At the first client's main entry, you approach a freshly painted high-gloss yellow door flanked by flowerpots brimming with freshly watered flowers. The sconce by the door is free of cobwebs, and the light comes on brightly as you approach at dusk. The house numbers are large and easy to read, and the welcome mat is freshly swept. The family tends to use a second entrance that goes through the garage and straight into the laundry room, where the floors are scrubbed and the walls are freshly painted. A recently vacuumed doormat inside the garage door catches extra dirt, and a series of cubbies capture shoes and coats. Recycle bins are handy so that junk mail never makes it into the house, and this year's calendar smiles brightly from the wall.

At the second client's main entry, the door paint is peeling, the door panels are crusted with grime, and a faded holiday wreath greets visitors even though it's early summer. The plants in the neglected pot are long dead from lack of water. The house numbers are small and so closely match the color of the house that you can't read them. This home also has a second door that the family enters through the garage into the laundry room, where the dirty vinyl floor is covered in mismatched shoes, and dust bunnies mix with lost socks by the dryer. The walls haven't been painted since the house was built, so the door frames are covered in greasy handprints, as is the paint around the light switches and door handle. A three-year-old calendar is thumbtacked to the wall, and a pile of junk mail perches precariously on top of the washer next to the laundry pile.

Beyond the superficial visual differences, the more important distinction between these entries is in how they make you feel as you enter. Every single day you'd either walk into a home that greets you with a smile and reminds you that your hard work has paid off, or into a home that meets you with a frown and makes you wonder why you bother. The care and setup of your house says either "welcome home" or "I give up" (or even "go away").

The entry to your home can't help but send you a daily message. A cluttered coat rack may imply that you have no boundaries and no ability to filter what is allowed into your life. A pile of stuff you meant to take to Goodwill months ago may suggest that you can't commit to letting go. Certainly you deserve a better "welcome home!"

What are you letting into your life?

SEEING YOURSELF REFLECTED IN YOUR HOME

**"The condition of my home is the
condition of my mind."
—Emily Martiniuk**

In her book *House as a Mirror of Self,* Clare Cooper Marcus illustrates how the home can give external clues to what is happening internally:

> How can you begin to identify and understand a changing image of yourself through your relationship with the environment? There are a number of cues to look for. One would be a subtle or perhaps nagging dissatisfaction with your current dwelling-place. You may find yourself reluctant to spend time there or to invite friends over. One woman I worked with, for example, after a divorce and the departure of her children for college, found herself increasingly alienated from the master bedroom. When she finally converted it into a study and created a new bedroom in a smaller former guest room, her life as a woman in her own right—neither wife nor mother—took a positive and creative turn. Another cue would be an unwillingness to personalize, decorate, or put any "mark" on your home. You may leave walls bare though you have plenty of pictures or photos you could put up. You may . . . leave belongings in boxes, unwilling perhaps to admit you are here to stay.

Both of my clients Marissa and Grace were unhappy with their current lives and therefore unwilling to commit to their current living situations. Marissa so desperately wanted to become a wife and mother that she refused to accept her current situation as a successful lawyer living single in a beautiful apartment with a gorgeous view. She'd lived there for five years and it looked like she'd moved in a month ago. Meanwhile my client Grace hated that she'd had to move to a smaller place in order to relaunch her life and business, having grown accustomed to having a large home and plenty of money. She resisted personalizing the space or making it feel remotely like home. Both Marissa and Grace neglected the spaces where they lived because they resented their situations and wanted something they didn't feel their homes provided. Once we worked together and they both put roots down in those bachelorette spaces, everything started to shift. They started to feel "at home," started feeling and behaving more grounded, and life started to align with their new way of living. Marissa found, and married, a wonderful man. Grace started attracting clients to her business and reestablished financial abundance.

SEEING YOUR HOME WITH NEW EYES

"We first make our habits, and then our habits make us." —John Dryden

Of course, it isn't as simple as "if A, then B." Living amid clutter doesn't mean you are afraid of letting go and facing truth, but it *can* mean that. Hanging art won't necessarily flood your life with instant positivity, but it *can* do that. The process of looking at our homes as mirrors of ourselves is a tool to use as part of an honest evaluation. Our choices—in words, clothes, friends—all the things we surround ourselves with, and the way we treat ourselves and allow ourselves to be treated, signal what is going on inside our minds. Because we react to, and mirror, our surroundings, changing them will, by design, help us change ourselves. Open up to change by altering the environments in which you work, live, love, and play.

The things that surround us in our homes signal what is going on in our minds.

We have to treat ourselves the way we wish to be treated by others, and that includes living in a situation that is healthful and supportive. When we let things fall apart around us, and accommodate things that are shabby, broken, and dangerous instead of demanding better for ourselves, we send out a message to the universe that we are not worthy, that we do not deserve anything better than what we have. Those messages are reinforced every day when we struggle against a closet door that won't slide open easily, or we look into a broken mirror each morning, or we use pliers to press the lever on the toaster because the handle broke off months ago. If your friend could afford a new toaster and yet you saw how she struggled with the broken one every morning, you would probably encourage her to get rid of that frustrating old appliance. Don't you deserve the same consideration? It can start by changing out something as simple as one burnt-out lightbulb. Shine a light on a new, improved life.

THE GOOD, THE BAD, AND THE FAMILIAR

"Better the devil you know than the devil you don't." —Jack Heath, *The Lab*

Why, then, do we remain stuck in frustrating situations and unpleasant spaces for so long? The reason is simple: We cling to our habits because they do something for us, they serve a purpose. We keep conditions around us static because they are familiar, comfortable. To behave in a new way, the need for something new must outweigh the need for what we have now. Oftentimes, even though we *say* we want something new, it's more that we think we *should* want something new. In reality we'd rather stick with what we know.

To behave in a new way the need for something different must outweigh the comfort of what we currently have.

Clutter can be comforting if it keeps you from having to face the truth (like sorting through the stuff from your childhood or addressing all the disappointing purchases you've made). For some people, a messy house protects them because it means they don't have to engage socially. (What better excuse *not* to have someone over than if the house isn't "ready"?) A closed-off entry prevents you from inviting anyone in. An unusable kitchen excuses an unhealthy lifestyle. An office-turned-storage room stops you from launching a freelance business. A TV-focused living room frees you from facing uncomfortable conversations within the family. A kid-overrun bedroom excuses the lack of intimacy in your marriage.

If you are ready for a more honest life, it will mean changing habits. It will mean changing what is around you. At first it may be deeply uncomfortable. In *You Can Heal Your Life*, Louise Hay maintains that "sometimes when we try to release a pattern, the whole situation seems to get worse for a while. This is not a bad thing. It is a sign that the situation is beginning to move. Our affirmations are working, and we need to keep going."

IN CASE OF A CHANGE IN CABIN AIR PRESSURE, PUT ON YOUR OWN MASK FIRST

Treating yourself well and recognizing your own self-worth may feel self-indulgent. Many of my clients waited until they were empty nesters simply because they didn't feel it was "right" to have a bedroom they loved or a kitchen that worked while they were raising their kids. Perhaps you don't have the financial freedom to undergo a $75,000 kitchen remodel while also paying teenage car insurance rates, but at least find the means to create a soothing bedroom—a place to rest and connect intimately with your partner—to build the reserves you need to be the kind of parent you want to be. It is not self-indulgent to take care of yourself. It is an investment in your family and will teach your kids that it is okay to take time for themselves when life gets stressful. What a precious lesson and gift to share with your children.

COLOR YOURSELF INTO A NEW STATE OF HAPPINESS

> **"When you feel good you uplift your life and you uplift the world."—Rhonda Byrne**

Changing your self-image is the hardest work of all, because the voices in your head are often the loudest, and no one else can hear them and tell them to be quiet for you. That is why the home can be such a powerful tool for transforming your idea of self-worth. "When you work on your home, you are working on yourself, and when you change your home, you are changing yourself," says Maxwell Gillingham-Ryan in *Apartment Therapy*. Instead of beating your head against the proverbial wall trying to change your thoughts, focus your energy on changing the paint color on your walls. Having been there myself, I can tell you that a remarkable transformation can happen in your heart as you watch the walls go from one color to another. Later, as you scrub the paint out of your hair and out from under your fingernails, you'll find yourself uncovering not just a new room, but a new you.

Little actions start the gears moving on a beautiful cycle of renewal. Hang a fresh pair of curtains. Scrub the tile so it gleams. Rid the closet of all your ill-fitting clothes. Replace all the burnt-out lightbulbs. I guarantee you'll start to feel better. You'll hold your head a little higher. You'll smile just a little more easily. Then someone will smile back. And you'll have started a chain reaction that can only lead to more positivity, and help not only yourself but also everyone you touch. That's about as selfless as it gets.

OUR HOMES, OURSELVES

Can I tell you some of the things I love about my home? In my bathroom I have light sconces on either side of the mirror so that the light never accentuates bags under my eyes. The walls of my bedroom are painted deep navy blue, and I have blackout curtains over my windows so that I can easily close out the world and get a really deep night of sleep. In my living room I have several adorable creatures: an owl pillow, a stuffed leather frog, and the coolest unicorn skull made by a local potter.

Why do each of these things matter? Because they bring me joy. I am hard enough on my body as it is: I don't need bathroom lighting that adds ten years to my face. (You know how horrible you feel after looking at your body in a bad dressing room under fluorescent lights? Bad bathroom lighting does that to you daily.) So when I remodeled I chose warm side lighting rather than harsh overhead lighting. Because I chose deep, sensual, rich colors for the walls and light-controlling curtains, it's me, not the neighborhood streetlights, that controls my go-to-sleep experience. When I get a good night of sleep, my world is a better place. I have more energy, more joy, and much more patience! And the creatures in my living room? They simply make me smile!

The personal things in our homes matter because they bring us joy.

In a home that says "You are worthwhile," the spaces are well-maintained, updated, clean and, most importantly, *personalized*. Think back to your childhood. Didn't you like to create private no-boys-allowed clubs, cardboard box homes, and pillow forts? Long before most of us ever became homeowners, we defined spaces for ourselves and they had a holiness, a sacredness that was not allowed to be crossed. In *House as a Mirror of Self*, Clare Cooper Marcus writes, "Whether these places were called forts, dens, houses, hideaways, or clubhouses, whether they were in the home or were found, modified, or constructed, they all seem to serve similar psychological and social purposes—place in which separation from adults was sought, in which fantasies could be acted out, and in which the very environment itself could be molded and shaped to one's own needs. *This is the beginning of the act of dwelling, or claiming one's place in the world.*" This early recognition of the human need to claim space by changing the environment appears to be nearly instinctual in children. In your adult life, reluctance to make that mark, to influence your space, may be a sign that you don't feel like you belong, that you don't feel confident enough about your own self-identity to make that mark.

A ROOM OF YOUR OWN

> **"You should feel beautiful and you should feel safe. What you surround yourself with should bring you peace of mind and peace of spirit." —Stacy London**

Starting in childhood when we build forts and get to control who may come in and who may not, we all have an important need to control some space. A private spot where we can be alone. Long after we stop creating our fantasy play spaces, we still have a need for a room or at least a corner where we imagine no one can find us, or disturb us. Where we can be left in peace. This can be especially important for a mother who feels compelled to make her children her whole universe. Without a place to call her own, this mom can lose any sense of self separate from the kids, which can be suffocating for the children and disorienting for her, especially as the kids grow and pull away and seek to define themselves in the world.

Many of us fondly remember our first place. Why, despite the cockroaches, the broken lock, the creepy guy down the hall, does it always have a special golden glow in your memory? Because it was the first time you got to be king or queen of your castle, featherer of your own nest. In your childhood home, many decisions were made for you. But in your first place, there is no one but you to determine how you shall live, when you will come home, what your walls will say about this new, unbounded, free-to-fly you.

SAY YES TO NEW ADVENTURES

> "Learn to adjust yourself to the conditions you have to endure, but make a point of trying to alter or correct conditions so that they are most favorable to you."
> —William Frederick Book

We know children need to express their emerging identities, separate from parents or siblings, through the personalization of space. But of course growth, change, and development doesn't stop with childhood. It continues on as we land our first job, partner with a lover, raise children, send the kids away from home, retire. With each transition we need to continually express our emerging identities. If your house stays stuck for two decades, your spirit does too. If you choose not to make changes, are you afraid of losing what you had, fearful that nothing better will come along? That you will lose your youth? Perhaps you fear that letting go of that ratty old recliner means that your bachelor days are over and if it goes, your youth does too. Is it possible that you're afraid the best days of your life have passed by? There must be a balance between holding on and letting go, and you must develop faith that you are wonderful enough to have another amazing chapter of your life story in you. You are not old news.

> ## With each transition you embark upon another amazing chapter in your life story. You are *not* old news.

It can be scary to let go of who you were, or who you once believed yourself to be. It can be a lot less scary to play with the edges of those possibilities by changing your environment. The very ordinariness of new sheets or new posters on the walls is exactly what makes them so powerful. By making those little changes you can slowly, step by step, walk out of your old life and into a new one. In *The Secret*, Rhonda Byrne reminds us, "You get to fill the blackboard of your life with whatever you want. If you have filled it in with baggage from the past, wipe it clean. Erase everything from the past that does not serve you, and be grateful it brought you to this place now and to a new beginning. You have a clean slate, and you can start over—right here, right now. Find your joy and live it."

Activity 46. Old Baggage: Assumptions, Power, Procrastination, Denial, and Fear

In this exercise we'll explore what may be holding you back from change.

As you read through this list of statements I have heard from clients, mark any that resonate with you:

Beliefs and assumptions: What excuses are you hiding behind?

- ☐ Trying to declutter won't do any good; my husband won't let go of anything.
- ☐ I've failed before; it'll just get bad again.
- ☐ I'm not good at decorating; I have no taste.
- ☐ I have to keep this because my sister/mom/friend/mother-in-law gave it to me.
- ☐ I have to keep this because it was my grandmother's/daughter's.
- ☐ My partner doesn't see the need for change, and so he won't let me make changes.
- ☐ This clutter isn't really affecting my family/relationships/health/work.
- ☐ If I make changes, my mom/husband/kids won't understand.

- ☐ Whatever I do, it won't be enough.
- ☐ Whatever I do, it needs to be perfect.
- ☐ It's not right to get rid of these things.
- ☐ I might need these things some day.
- ☐ "They" might need these things some day.
- ☐ It's selfish to focus on creating space for me.
- ☐ It's selfish to create a beautiful home when a lot of people don't even have a home.
- ☐ It's too much work; it's too expensive; it will take too long.
- ☐ I'm just not an organized person.

Question: If your best friend were to say these things to you, what advice would you give her?

_____
_____
_____
_____
_____

Power struggles: Who or what are you allowing to have power over you?

- ☐ I'm waiting for the right time.
- ☐ This isn't my forever home.
- ☐ I don't own this home.
- ☐ I moved into my new partner's home, and I can't change anything.
- ☐ I don't have the right coach/book/class/tools.
- ☐ My home is too small.
- ☐ My home is too big.
- ☐ I am not healthy enough.
- ☐ I am too tired.
- ☐ I can't get time off work.
- ☐ It's not my stuff.
- ☐ It's just part of having kids.
- ☐ It's just part of being married.
- ☐ They have to change first.
- ☐ As soon as I get _____ then I'll do it.
- ☐ I don't want to hurt them.
- ☐ Only rich people live in nice homes.

Question: If your best friend were giving up this kind of control over her own life, what advice would you give her?

_____

_____

_____

_____

_____

Procrastination: How are you excusing your delay?
- ☐ I'll do it later.
- ☐ I can't think right now.
- ☐ I don't have time right now.
- ☐ It would take too much time away from my work/parenting.
- ☐ I have too many other things to do.
- ☐ I'll do it as soon as I get through with _____
- ☐ I'll do it as soon as I get back from _____
- ☐ The time isn't right; it's too late/it's too soon.

Question: If your best friend were making these excuses, what advice would you give her?

_____

_____

_____

_____

_____

Denial: Is your head in the sand?
- ☐ There isn't a problem.
- ☐ It's not my problem.
- ☐ I can't do anything about this problem.
- ☐ Changing things wouldn't do any good.
- ☐ The problem will go away if I ignore it.

Question: If your best friend were hiding from the truth, what advice would you give her?

_____

_____

_____
_____
_____

Fear: What are you hiding from?
- ☐ I'm not ready yet.
- ☐ I might fail.
- ☐ They might reject me.
- ☐ What will they think?
- ☐ I'm afraid to tell my spouse things are not working.
- ☐ I might get hurt.
- ☐ I may have to change.
- ☐ It might cost money.
- ☐ I would rather get a divorce first.
- ☐ I don't want anyone to know I have a problem.
- ☐ I don't want to talk about it.
- ☐ I don't have the energy.
- ☐ It's too hard.
- ☐ I wouldn't be perfect.
- ☐ I might lose my friends.
- ☐ It might hurt my image.
- ☐ I'm not good enough.

Question: If your best friend shared these fears with you, what advice would you give her?

_____
_____
_____
_____
_____

Activity 47. Questions to Identify and Defeat Limiting Beliefs

Choose three to six statements from Activity 46, the ones that really struck a chord in your heart. List them in the blanks below and answer the questions that follow. For example, you might have resonated with:

- I might fail.
- Changing things wouldn't do any good.

- I don't have time right now.
- The problem will go away if I ignore it.
- My home is too small.
- It's selfish to focus on creating space for me.

Coaches who focus on identifying and eliminating these kinds of internalized beliefs like to challenge their clients with this simple question: "Is this really true?" *Just because you believe it doesn't necessarily make it true.* Now let's explore how you will defeat your limiting beliefs.

My top six "true" statements from Activity 46:

1. _____
2. _____
3. _____
4. _____
5. _____
6. _____

Look at the above statements. Are they true? Are they really true? What would happen if they were *not* true?

_____
_____
_____

What dream are these thoughts preventing me from realizing? How are these pessimistic thoughts protecting me?

_____
_____
_____

Who in my family used to (or still does) makes similar statements? How do I feel when I hear this from other people?

_____
_____
_____

Are these beliefs keeping me from obtaining what I want? Does that feel safe?

_____

_____

_____

Do I value something that contradicts what I say I want for my home and my life?

_____

_____

_____

What "failures" in my past have "proven" these statements? Am I allowing these so-called failures to keep me from trying something new?

_____

_____

_____

What black-and-white philosophies do these statements reveal that keep me frozen in a passive way?

_____

_____

_____

Review your answers and decide if that is how you wish to live the rest of your life story. You can't rewrite the past, but you sure do have control over the next chapter. You are the author of your own story, and you can write the words of power and positivity on the walls of your very own home!

Activity 48. I Feel Pretty

Feeling pretty can do wonders for your posture and your confidence and affect everything from your health to your career. Walk through your home, room by room. As you walk through, identify things that make you smile, and things that make you cringe.

Think of ways you can increase the number of happiness-inducing elements. Eliminate at least one cringe-worthy element in the next forty-eight hours.

In the next forty-eight hours I will eliminate:

_____

_____

_____

_____

_____

TO SUM UP

The colors we choose, the objects and books we place on our shelves, the pictures and posters we put on the walls—we select them because of what they add to our lives and homes, both functionally and aesthetically. But the items and elements are also projections, or "messages" from the unconscious, the same way that our dreams contain such messages. What messages are we letting our home send us every morning when we wake up and every evening as we go to sleep?

With all the self-help books we read, all the diets we endure, all the affirmations we repeat, if we can foster the chance for a wonderful life by changing our environment, why wouldn't we do it? If we can create a space where it is easier to feel good, to feel aligned with our values, to feel closer to our spiritual source, why wouldn't we do it?

Remember, you don't have to know how. You don't have to see the whole path. You only have to take the next step. Louise Hay offers this mantra: "I realize I have created this condition, and I am now willing to release the pattern in my consciousness that is responsible for this condition." She then acknowledges that once someone embraces a readiness to change, they may find that they're scared—they don't know _how_ to do the releasing. It's okay to be scared. Accepting change doesn't take knowing all the answers, and waiting for all the answers is just another excuse for not moving forward. Pass through the resistance and take a small step forward. Remember this: "The journey of a thousand miles begins with one step."

Conclusion

"As above, so below. As within, so without."
—*The Emerald Tablet of Hermes*
Trismegistus

IN THE HERMETIC SPIRITUAL TRADITION, whatever happens on any level of reality (physical, emotional, or mental) also happens on every other level. That means our outer reality is a reflection of our inner reality, and we can shift our inner reality by making changes to our outer reality. No matter what your spiritual path, it is clear that when your life is congruent, meaning that your walk and your talk or your prayers and your actions are in alignment, you can be whole and complete.

If you are *not* walking your talk, awareness of that dissonance is the first key to change. Once you have committed to change, the next step is to gather the tools you need to create change. Your home can be one of the easiest and most powerful tools in your journey toward a new way of living. If you have worked through the exercises in this book, you have developed that awareness.

Now that you've started to see your home with new eyes, the key is to take action. But not just any action—*inspired* action. Have intention behind your work. When you know what you want to receive in your life, whether it is new love, more wealth, better family dynamics, improved health, or a livelier social life, and you take action to support that intent, you open the channel for the universe to bring goodness into your life. On the other hand, action without intent is just busy work and won't necessarily get you where you want to go.

THE NOT-SO-SECRET KEYS TO SUCCESS

**"Take the first step in faith. You don't
have to see the whole staircase. Just
take the first step."
—Martin Luther King Jr.**

When I work with clients who are ready to create a home that really and truly supports their life, we use many of the same tools you'll find in any how-to book on organizing, decorating, and designing. It's a lot like dieting: the basic rules never change, and there are no secrets that only designers know. It's just a matter of applying the guidelines around proportions, textures, contrast, etc., in a way that creates a pleasing space, just as losing weight is technically just a matter of planning low-calorie, high-nutrition meals and making exercise a regular habit.

Of course we all know that losing weight isn't quite that easy, and keeping the weight off long term works only when you understand *why* you are losing weight, *who* you are losing weight for, and *what you will gain* from all that effort. Going on a diet without that strong foundation generally leads to disappointment, but going on a diet *with* that strong foundation can inspire a brand new lifestyle and lead to long-term, healthy change.

The same goes for feeling dissatisfied with your home's appearance. If you update based only on the latest trends, you are missing the step that ensures you will end up creating a home that is not only pleasing to the eye but also nurturing to the soul.

The key is to start with the *why*. Ask yourself, "Why do I need to make a change to this space?" Consider your final destination. How do you want your life to be different after you invest your time and money in your home? Will it pay off in an emotional and a supportive way? Before you lift a paintbrush, take time to figure out what you want from your home and your life, and what you want to eliminate from your home and your life.

Creating a home that supports you isn't a one-time event. Just like exercising or meditating, keeping your home alive must become a regular part of your life. Instead of spring cleaning because you "should," do it with intention, focusing on what you want to invite into your life in the coming summer, and what you want to leave behind from the winter. Every action is guided by your goals; energy is never wasted on useless action; and you are rewarded for your efforts by achieving your bigger goals. Tending your home becomes an emotional exercise, not one fraught with frustration and futility.

Activity 49. Lighten the Load: Four Weeks to Lighter Living

When I introduce the Happy Starts at Home program to my clients, we use many of the exercises in this book to identify what changes are needed. And we create a Take-Action Plan to divide the work into manageable bites. You can do this too. Complete the following outline over the course of a week or a month, depending on the amount of time you have and the size of the area you are addressing. Imagine you have four weeks, and you spend one day a week in this way:

Day 1: Have a conversation with your home and set your intentions

On your first day, you won't clean, organize, or paint anything. You will have a conversation with your home and set clear intentions for your project. Look at Activity 1, the Wheel of Life, and identify the aspect of your life you want to improve.

I would like to improve my _____ life.

Write a letter to your home in two parts. In part one, express in writing how your home makes you feel about that aspect of your life.

Dear Home: The way you make me feel about my _____ life is:

_____

_____

_____

_____

_____

_____

_____

_____

_____

_____

Now for part two: Sit quietly for a moment and listen, then write as if your home were responding to you. What choices could have been made to let the house support you better in that way? Take as much time as you need, but try to write for at least ten minutes.

Dear Person Who Lives Here: I am sorry I am not able to support you in the way that you need. I might be able to better support you if:

_____

_____

_____

_____

_____

_____

_____

_____

_____

_____

Think of a space that makes you feel good about that aspect of your life. Now imagine yourself there—how it sounds, feels, looks, even tastes. Take ten more minutes and write about five key differences between the space you have just visited in your mind and the space in which you currently live.

_____

_____

_____

_____

_____

Answer the following questions as specifically as you can. If you could wave a magic wand and—*poof!*—live in your perfect space, how would your life be different? Relate it to the aspect of life you want to change:

If I were to make the changes needed so that my home was more like the perfect, nurturing space of my dreams, if it supported me and made me feel powerful and wonderful in my _____ life, this is how my life would be different: _____

_____

_____

_____

_____

_____

Does that vision of your future motivate you? If not, go back through the activity and give yourself permission to think a little bigger. But if your vision *does* motivate you, you've just defined your intention and your reason for the effort you are about to expend.

Next, make a contract with yourself:

> Going forward, I am going to feel powerful, supported, and inspired in my _____ life, and my home is going to help create the change I need to accomplish that. As I embark on this journey, I will continually ask, "Does everything in my home make me feel fantastic, clear, confident about my _____ life?" That which does not support me will go.
>
>   Signed _____

Finally, the last task for this day is to paraphrase as much of that contract and intention as you wish in big, bold letters on a large piece of paper, and tape it to the wall in the room you are about to tackle. This way you can have a constant reminder of why you are spending your precious time on this project while you do the work. It will motivate you to keep going when it's hard, and help you avoid getting sucked into a vortex of nostalgia, regret, or grief as you uncover things that are uncomfortable. Be as creative as you like—use glitter and fancy pens if that's your style—just don't get stuck on making it perfect. Get it done and get it up on the wall so it's waiting for you on Day 2. Action and accomplishment are keys to the success of the Happy Starts at Home program.

Day 2: Make a plan

Your project today is to make a plan of executable action. Decide the following:

What room am I tackling? _____
What needs to change?

_____

_____

_____

_____

_____

What are the top-three easiest items to change in this room?

_____

_____

_____

What are the two hardest items to change in this room?

_____

_____

What resources do I need?

_____

_____

_____

Who needs to be involved?

_____

_____

_____

Now accomplish the top-three easiest items, and then call your resources and the folks who need to be involved. Get your ducks in a row, so to speak, because on Day 3 you'll change the two hardest items in the room.

Day 3: Execute the big stuff
Today is the day you pull on the work gloves and get the big stuff done. Hopefully you've called in and collected the resources you need to accomplish one or both of the hardest things in the room. Now take action! Depending on the kind of project you are undertaking, see the resources at happystartsathome.com to help you take on the project without being overwhelmed or consumed by fear, frustration, or nostalgia.

Note: You don't have to *finish* the project on Day 3. Do enough to give yourself a huge sense of accomplishment.

Day 4: Bless and celebrate your progress

This is a day to focus on celebrating. You may not be done yet (because, of course, your home is an organic, living space and, like you, is a work in progress), but you have faced a challenge and made headway. Congratulations! Now take a minute for reflection and gratitude:

1. **Reflect.** Pour yourself a cup of tea or a glass of champagne and complete the following:

What I accomplished:

_____
_____
_____
_____
_____

Because I accomplished that, I feel:

_____
_____
_____
_____
_____

2. **Share the celebration.** Call, text, or email a friend and tell them what you've accomplished and how it makes you feel. Be sure to choose someone who will be happy for you and not diminish your achievement or demand more of you.

3. **Express gratitude.** Say thank you to anyone who helped. That can include your partner for clearing out junk, your kids for playing in their rooms, your sister for watching the kids, your boss for giving you a day off, even the folks at the local home-improvement store who helped you find stuff you needed.

4. **Say thank you to your home.** Revisit the conversation you had with your home on Day 1 and write a new letter in two parts. First, acknowledge how your home made you feel about that aspect of your life you wished to change, and write the new feelings you are having now.

Dear Home: Before, you made me feel _____ about my
_____ life. Now that we have made these changes together, I feel:

_____

_____

_____

_____

_____

_____

_____

_____

_____

_____

Now sit quietly for a moment and listen, and write as if your home were responding to you:

Dear Person Who Lives Here: I am glad we have made these changes. I am now better able to support you because:

_____

_____

_____

_____

_____

5. Now that some of the "noise" is gone, evaluate how you want to move forward, and ask the universe for clarity about what needs to happen next. To help you along, here are some of my past clients' revelations:

- Once we finished making over the living room, James recognized that he needed to address the office. Doing an "easy" room first had proven that it *could* be done; he *could* love his home and life more. It gave him the courage to take on a "harder" room. The result? When we decluttered the office, he felt free to start his own business and soon had hired two employees of his own.
- Once we finished decorating her downtown apartment, Marissa knew her next step would be to invite new friends over and start exploring

a new romantic life for herself. Within a year she'd met and married the man of her dreams.

- When Mary finished the remodel of her kitchen, her next step was to start preparing meals at home. She subsequently lost over 100 pounds (and has kept it off for more than three years). Her doctor's warning of impending death became a distant memory.

You've made some changes to your home. What is it you want to tackle next? What needs to happen next in your home or your life?

_____

_____

_____

_____

_____

_____

_____

_____

_____

_____

If your project is not done, revisit your writing from Day 1, re-identify the easy and hard stuff as in Day 2, and then take two more cycles addressing the easy stuff, and then the tough stuff. Repeat as needed.

A NEW WAY OF LIVING

> **"I can hardly wait for tomorrow, it means
> a new life for me each and every day."**
> **—Stanley Kunitz**

Remember, just as you should never stop exploring, learning, and growing, your home will never be "done." This pattern of setting an intention, picking the low-hanging fruit, tackling the hard stuff with help, and celebrating should become a habit. Perhaps you'll make it a monthly or quarterly ritual. Pick at least four times on your calendar for the year when you will begin with Day 1, then let the process unfold naturally. You do not have to do it all at once, or perfectly. You can't. The point is simply to take action. Remember, the most important step is step one, setting the intention, knowing *why* it matters to you.

Another reminder: you do *not* have to go it alone. It is okay to seek the help of professional organizers, decorators, and contractors. Just be sure that you've set your intentions first and that your helpers are eager and excited to focus on that goal, and not a goal of their own.

BRING IN YOUR TEAM

> **"By asking for help it's not that you're weak, it's not that you're anything like that, it's just allowing somebody else to give their gift." —Marjean Holden**

It can feel overwhelming to do these things on your own, and that is why people reach out for help. Working with me, or working with another coach, or even partnering with a friend, creates accountability and helps you keep perspective. Another person's issues, piles, and problems somehow never feel as insurmountable as our own, and by helping a friend tackle her project, you might discover some tools to help you with yours too.

For resources, check out the Checklist for Easy Decluttering, Order of Action for Your Kitchen Remodel, and other tips on the blog at happystarts athome.com.

HOME: THE HEART OF YOUR HAPPINESS

> **"A home fulfills many needs: (it is) a place of self-expression, a vessel of memories, a refuge from the outside world, a cocoon where we can feel nurtured and let down our guard." —Clare Cooper Marcus, *House as a Mirror of Self***

Life is filled with challenges, and it takes courage to do what needs to be done and change what needs to change. Sometimes, instead of taking the challenge head on—asking your boss for a raise, eliminating sugar from your diet, finding a life partner—you can first shift things in your home to create an environment that will support the new goal, give you the courage for the bigger challenge, and send a message to the universe that you are ready to receive that new money, new body, and new love.

Sometimes getting away from it all and returning with new perspective helps you see your home with new eyes. That is what happened for Winifred Gallagher in her book *House Thinking:* "Like many a traveler, I reconsidered my dwelling with a fresh eye and saw that it had become both dysfunctional and dull. Oh, the house seemed all right at first glance, but after years of routine housekeeping and not much house thinking, it wasn't really supporting our needs, much less engaging our minds or delighting our hearts as it should." It took an extended trip overseas, and a chance to write a book about the psychological impact of home, for Gallagher to think about her home from a "feel-good rather than merely look-good perspective."

Similarly, I hope that by reading this book you see new ways in which your life could be working better and your home can support you. After all, the purpose of having a house is to *live* your *life* out of it.

May your home be a blessing and the foundation of your extraordinary life.

May it be happy and bring you joy.

Selected Bibliography

Here is a partial list of the resources I have found useful in writing and speaking about the Happy Starts at Home program.

Arnold, Jeanne, Anthony P. Graesch, Enzo Ragazzini, and Elinor Ochs. *Life at Home in the Twenty-first Century: 32 Families Open Their Doors.* 1st ed. Los Angeles: Cotsen Institute of Archaeology Press, 2012.

Byrne, Rhonda. *The Secret.* New York: Atria Books/Beyond Words, 2006.

Chiazzari, Suzy. *Our Place: Improve Your Home, Improve Your Relationship.* New York: Watson-Guptill, 2002.

Csikszentmihalyi, Mihaly. *Flow: The Psychology of Optimal Experience.* 1st ed. New York: Harper Perennial, 1990.

Gallagher, Winifred. *House Thinking: A Room-by-Room Look at How We Live.* New York: HarperCollins, 2006.

— —. *The Power of Place: How Our Surroundings Shape Our Thoughts, Emotions, and Actions.* New York: HarperPerennial, 1994.

Gillingham-Ryan, Maxwell. *Apartment Therapy: The Eight-Step Home Cure.* New York: Bantam Dell, 2006.

Goode, Randa. "A Little Messiness Never Hurt Anyone," March 10, 2014, http://www.randagoode.com/a-little-messiness-never-hurt-anyone/.

Hay, Louise. *You Can Heal Your Life.* Carlsbad, CA: Hay House, 1984.

Jameson, Marni. *The House Always Wins: Create the Home You Love—Without Busting Your Budget*. Cambridge, MA: Da Capo Press, 2008.

Marcus, Clare Cooper. *House as a Mirror of Self: Exploring the Deeper Meaning of Home*. Lake Worth, FL: Nicolas-Hays, 2006.

Pink, Daniel H. *A Whole New Mind: Why Right-Brainers Will Rule the Future*. New York: Penguin/Riverhead Books, 2005.

Shaw, Judith. "Why Is Creative Expression Important to the Human Soul?," *Life on the Edge* [blog], May 1, 2009, https://judithshaw.wordpress.com.

About the Author

Certified design psychology coach and interior designer Rebecca West helps create spaces that support, rather than sabotage, the people who live in them. She believes a beautiful home is not about the sofa or what's on trend, it's about what works for your family and fits your lifestyle. It's about having a home that makes you happy.

After living the nomadic life of a military child, Rebecca has created her own happy home in the Pacific Northwest, where the natural environment and unfussy Seattle lifestyle influence her clean, fresh, livable designs.

The popular designer, blogger, and speaker showcases her before-and-after photos at happystartsathome.com and invites readers to share their home transformation stories at design@rebeccawestinteriors.com.

MORE GREAT READS
FROM BOOKTROPE

Eat in Not Out-The Learn-How-to-Cook Book Without Recipes **by Melinda Hinson Neely** (How-to/Food & Nutrition) Learn to set up a kitchen, buy the right food, prepare simple and delicious meals, and eat healthy and economically with this helpful guide.

The Essential Stay-at-Home Mom Manual **by Shannon Hyland-Tassava** (How-to) A clinical psychologist and stay-at-home mom provides solutions for better emotional and physical health, and practical strategies for making at-home motherhood easier and more fun.

Don't Pee on My Sofa! And Other Things to Laugh About **by C. Suzanne Bates** (Humor) Tips and Strategies for Embracing Life After 50 from AgingButDANGEROUS.com®

Ride of Your Life **by Ran Zilca** (Memoir/Self-help) A guide to inner peace, composed over a 6,000 miles contemplative motorcycle ride, while meeting with experts like Deepak Chopra and Phil Zimbardo.

Would you like to read more books like these?
Subscribe to **runawaygoodness.com**, get a free ebook for signing up,
and never pay full price for an ebook again.

Discover more books and learn about our
new approach to publishing at **www.booktrope.com**.